HITCHHIKER'S
GUIDE TO EVANGELISM

HITCHHIKER'S GUIDE TO EVANGELISM

Bill Tenny-Brittian

CHALICE
PRESS

ST. LOUIS, MISSOURI

Cover art: Elizabeth Wright with images from FotoSearch
Cover and interior design: Elizabeth Wright

Visit Chalice Press on the World Wide Web at
www.chalicepress.com

10 9 8 7 6 5 4 3 2 1   08 09 10 11 12

Library of Congress Cataloging–in–Publication Data

Tenny-Brittian, Bill.
  Hitchhiker's guide to evangelism / By Bill Tenny-Brittian.
    p. cm.
  ISBN 978-0-8272-1454-5
  1. Evangelistic work. 2. Witness bearing (Christianity) 3. Missions. I. Title.

BV3790.T44 2008
269'.2–dc22

2008044097

Printed in the United States of America

Contents

Acknowledgments and Dedication

This book would not have seen the light of day without the many Hitchhikers who have gently, and sometimes not so gently, guided me along this great and awesome adventure. My thanks to Pastor Dan Anderson and his wife Lori, wherever y'all are, who were the church planters of Highlands Christian Church in Kennewick, Washington, who nurtured the spark within me and fanned into flame my devotion to Jesus and my love for evangelism. Also my heartfelt thanks to Dr. Leroy Benefield, my evangelism professor, who kept sending me out into the harvest to share my faith.

And finally to my family. My wife Kris, who read, edited, commented, and kept me in front of the laptop (no mean task, I promise). And to my children Toni, Becky, Katrina, Shannon, and Britt, whose stories are interwoven in many ways throughout this book. I love you all and am grateful for your never-ending encouragement.

Our Once upon a Time

What kind of story are you living? Is it bigger than life? The great, grand story of a sweeping eternity with unending consequences? I don't know about you, but the story I tend to find myself in is less a story of the eternal and more the story of the mundane. Bills and budgets, kids and pets, parishioners and pills, hopes and dreams, but mostly wishful thinking.

It's the story of most of us. Jesus claimed he came to give us "life to the full" (Jn. 10:10), but take an honest look around the church. Do you discover *anyone* there whose life is so full of Christian excitement, passion, and joy that you'd want to trade lives?

Now don't get me wrong! Plenty of good and noble things are going on in the church. People can discover Jesus there. They find support in their times of crisis and camaraderie in their times of celebration. People are baptized, married, and buried in the church. All of that's good stuff.

But it hardly measures up to what the Bible promised. Where's the peace that passes understanding (Phil. 4:7)? The unspeakable joy (1 Pet. 1:8)? The excitement, the hopes, the fullness, and all those things that the Christian life was supposed to deliver?

For many of us, it seems as though we've been robbed. We set out with an exciting, life-empowering vision we believed God had written on our hearts; but we were left with the church. Our dreams were waylaid, and we traded out our hopes for something much less noble.

Trading Our Hopes for…the Church

Years ago, I set out to start a new church. God had painted a vision of a people gathered together in one accord to go forth and make disciples of the nation. In the vision, people focused on reaching the unreached above all else. Everything they did, every ministry opportunity, every mission event was designed and executed to invite the unchurched and the irreligious into their sphere of influence.

We started out great. I spent most of my time meeting new people. I joined the Chamber of Commerce to network with the business folks in the community. I joined Toastmasters and went to the Optimist club. I hung out at the local coffee shop and started conversations. I did all the right things. When we launched, the church was full of the previously unreached. I felt ecstatic. The next thing, I knew, was to disciple these folks so they could do what I'd been doing. So I preached. And I taught. And I visited the newly reached. And pretty soon, before I knew it, I was doing church.

Doing Church

Doing church involves visiting, meetings, sermon preparation, worship team practice, newsletter writing, budget reviews, weekly planning, local minister's meetings, denominational minister's meetings, continuing education, and putting out fires in the congregation.

With all that, who had time to meet new people, to build new relationships, and to reach the unreached? In no time at all, I found myself in the same boat as most clergy I know and most Christians as well. I didn't have any unchurched or unreached friends, and I didn't have the energy or the expendable time to do anything about it. I was stuck running amuck on the Möbius strip of doing church.

Trading Our Hopes for...a Cocoon

But the church isn't the only thing we trade our hopes for. We also trade our hopes for a cocoon. We often relate a cocoon to the metaphor of life after death, of resurrection with the cocoon representing death. I suppose that's true enough, because a caterpillar spins a cocoon around itself and morphs into a beautiful butterfly. The problem is, most Americans are crawling into their cocoons and, instead of morphing, are using it as a shell to keep safe and to stay isolated.

Consider that most of us don't actually see or speak to the attendant at the gas station anymore. We use our credit cards or our debit cards, get our gasoline, and zoom out without speaking to a soul. We use the drive-up—or the walk-up—ATM and avoid the lines (the people) and the company of the teller. Then there's the self-checkout line at the grocery store—another opportunity to avoid actual interaction with someone. Some of us are shopping online, even grocery shopping, so we avoid both cashiers and crowds. Many of us are doing the virtual office thing, so we don't even have to go to the workplace anymore: we get to avoid travel time, traffic delays, and meaningful interaction with our coworkers. We communicate via telephone, e-mail, and instant messages, never once seeing the face of those with whom we tersely communicate.

The list goes on. We spend more and more time in our home offices in front of our computers. We're using drive-ups, drive-ins, and drive-bys. Many of us leave our garages in the morning, zip to work, work in our cubical, and drive home. The garage door opens and swallows us, and we're safe and sound without having to interact with anybody on any sort of personal level.

Let's face it, we've become a people of isolation. Most people hardly know their neighbors, and a lot of us honestly don't want to know them. We simply don't have time to make new friends. We use our cars, our homes, and our time-saving conveniences as cocoons to protect us from the big, bad, crowded world. As a result, we don't know any unchurched or unreached people because we really don't know very many people at all—at least not well enough to know their spiritual state.

Trading Our Hopes for…Nothing

Quick, how many unchurched or unreached people do you call "friends"? Unchurched acquaintances count, but just barely.

One of the most common concerns I hear from those in the pews is that they have nothing in common with the unchurched, so they don't go out of their way to befriend them. You know the irreligious: they tell off-color jokes. They gossip. They drink, gamble, and carouse. You can't trust them. And besides, they don't want to talk about religion or the church.

You may be surprised when I tell you that this is pretty much the same view many unchurched folks have about Christians. Oh, maybe we don't get the off-color jokes or carousing accusations much (although we've been accused of these too); instead, they're replaced with indictments of being judgmental, bigoted, self-absorbed, dogmatic, irrelevant, outdated, and hypocritical. They think they have nothing in common with us either. Hmm.

But if we start hanging out with the unchurched, won't we be in danger of slipping and falling into sin? You know, bad apples and all that? Aren't we supposed to protect ourselves from "the world"?

Yes, we are supposed to protect ourselves from the world. But we do that by putting on the full armor of God, not by cocooning and avoidance. By almost all accounts, Jesus generally had a good time while he walked the earth. He got invited to the best parties, hung out with the most interesting people, and had lots of diverse friends from all walks of life—the rich, the poor, the respectable, and the very colorful. Where do you think you'd find Jesus on a Saturday night these days? A nightclub? A movie? A concert? You lose reality points if you answered a Saturday night choral sing at church. Jesus spent most of his time with his best buddies and the irreligious crowd. And he clearly had a good time being with them.

But most of us have nothing in common with the unchurched because we either don't know, or have forgotten, how to relate to them, which, of course, brings up the other nothing.

We have nothing to *say* to the unchurched and the irreligious. I know a number of Christians who intentionally hang out with the unchurched folks in their communities. They spend time with them after work; they go to the theater with them, have a beer after work, and so on. But when it comes to bringing up their faith, they don't know what to say. In some cases, it's an issue of not knowing *how* to bring faith up, but most of the time they don't know what to say because they don't have an answer to the question, "Why share my faith?"

On the other hand, some honestly don't have much faith to share— they're still babes in the faith themselves, even though they might have been in the church for years. They've made an intellectual or an emotional decision to join the church, but their lives haven't been transformed by a relationship with Jesus. They don't feel or behave any differently than they did before they became a Christian.

Rewriting Your Story

So what's your story? Too busy to make friends or interact with others? Unsure of your answer to *the* question? Don't know how to meet and interact with the unchurched crowd? Need some ideas on how to get others excited about sharing their faith story? Whatever story you find yourself in, it's only been written to this moment. You have the ability to change the way the next chapter reads and the ultimate end of your story. If you want to really make a difference with your faith, if you have a yearning to live the exciting life that Jesus promises, and if you want your life and your church to have an impact on your community, this book can help. Besides reading the book and looking over the questions at the end of each chapter, take a stab at the exercises. Be honest with your answers and consider trying a few of the ideas. It'll make a difference, I promise. It has in my life and in the lives of countless others who have chosen to write a new chapter in their life stories by offering the hope and promises Jesus provides.

A Word about Words

In this book I use some terms you might not immediately recognize. As an aid to get you onboard, I've listed and defined them here.

The Way: The Christian faith journey. Before we were called Christians in Antioch, we were called followers of the Way (Acts 9:2). We travel along the Way with Jesus as our guide.

Hitchhikers: A Hitchhiker is one who's accepted a ride from another. In our case, Hitchhikers are people who stuck out their thumb on the spiritual highway and were "picked up" by the Spirit. A slight detour in time and space and they find themselves traveling through life on the Way with Jesus. In other words, they're faithful Christians.

Wanderers: The people formerly know as "lost." These people don't know they're lost—they don't feel lost—but they are regularly found wandering aimlessly on the spiritual byways like "sheep without a shepherd."

Nomads: People who believe in Jesus, but haven't found a spiritual home. They are unchurched, but they claim Christianity as their faith.

Tourists: Churchgoers who are pretty much only interested in what they can get out of church. Consumers who don't invest much in the life of the congregation other than attending.

CHAPTER ONE

The Journey Begins

But how are they to call on one in whom they have not believed? And how are they to believe in one of whom they have never heard? And how are they to hear without someone to proclaim him? (Rom. 10:14, NRSV)

If you do a search of Amazon.com for books on evangelism, you'll discover over 10,000 books on the topic. Of course, that's only the beginning. Hundreds of evangelism newsletters are available from the Internet along with over a thousand evangelism seminars and workshops and untold millions of articles on the subject. So, why in the world do we need another book on evangelism?

Because of the Carols in the World

I met Carol at the café where I coached a small group of house-church pastors on Sunday mornings. Carol was a Washington State University student who tended to work in the back of the café, but I'd been slowly building a relationship with her for months. I bussed my own table, so I'd bump into her. I tried to keep track of events in her life so I could ask relevant questions. I made no secret about what I was doing every Sunday with the small gathering of men and women while we were having breakfast—nothing pushy, just an ordinary attempt at conversation.

Conversations tended to be polite small talk, "How was your week?" and so on. Until one Sunday when the Spirit opened a door. "I've never understood why the church excommunicates people. Why would they throw out the 'sinners' when they're the ones who need church the most?" Even roll-up industrial hanger doors at Boeing don't open any wider than that. By the time we'd finished chatting that Sunday, we'd explored several of the most common questions Wanderers ask:

- What about "other" religions?
- Why would a good God send people to hell?
- Why is there evil, and where did it come from?
- Why does God allow people to suffer?
- Why doesn't God intervene when bad things happen?
- Is Jesus *really* the only way?

Carol is just one of millions unreached or unchurched people in the United States and Canada,[1] but she's not the only one asking questions. These are common questions that the church to a large extent leaves unanswered. Carol is one of millions whom the church basically ignores. Oh sure, many churches run ads in the local newspapers announcing their weekly services. Other churches mass mail clever postcards that invite "Our Friends at 1201 Pacific Avenue" to drop by for coffee, doughnuts, and a message about life's purpose. But most congregations seem content with the "y'all come" style of marketing that takes aim at the 2 percent market share who are actually looking for a church. But what other choice is there? It's not in vogue to go randomly knocking on doors anymore, and by most accounts it's not very effective. Indeed, the negative impact that door-knocking evangelism creates on a skeptical public may far outweigh the few positive responses these evangelists get.

The Church Is Out of Practice

By and large, traditional one-on-one evangelism is unpracticed in the North American church. The results have devastated the North American church, where attendance losses continue to escalate. For instance, the church is losing over 2.5 million people per year and has been since 1991.[2] But there's a more serious issue than just church membership or attendance losses. Christianity in much of the West is declining in numbers: "There are 3,000 fewer Christians now than 24 hours ago."[3] If you do the math, that works out to over a million people a year leaving the faith—not the church, the faith. Now, admittedly, we have two issues here. First is the issue of why people are leaving the church and the faith. That's the subject for another book. The second issue, however, is that all of the church's evangelism efforts combined are working so poorly that we can't overcome the losses.

By now you may be asking, so what is working? Is no evangelism occurring in our churches? And of course, that's not the case. Many church members are working diligently in the harvest fields, sharing their faith with others, and introducing their friends, relatives, acquaintances, neighbors, coworkers, and everyone else to Jesus. Everyday, men, women, youth, and children are choosing to follow Jesus on the Way. The problem is, so few North American Christians are practicing evangelism that it takes an average of eighty-five church members one full year to bring one Wanderer to the faith.[4] Additionally, according to the *World Christian Encyclopedia*, the church spends $1,551,466 for each new convert.[5]

Okay, so much for the bad news. Let's look at some good news. First, *you* are reading this book. That's an indication there's still hope. The fact that people like you are trying to figure it out, trying to find some way to make a difference for the kingdom of God, means we may be about to change the trends. Second, you are reading *this* book. I wrote *The Hitchhiker's Guide to Evangelism* for one purpose and one purpose only: to get at the root of our hesitancy about sharing the greatest news on earth and to offer simple training that real people can use in their real lives. I'm not going to try to convince you to get out there and knock on doors, to strike up faith-sharing conversations with strangers, or whip up enthusiasm in your church to start an evangelism campaign. Instead, I promise to keep it simple, to remove as many obstacles as possible, and to keep you as close to your comfort zone as I can.

The Direction in This Chapter

With that said, let me introduce this chapter, because it's significantly different from all the rest. Consider this chapter your travel guide to the journey you're about to embark on. Now, before you take any trip you must first take care of some advanced planning. Most of the time, this planning is done so naturally you might not even be aware of the steps you take. For instance, before you go anywhere, in some manner you've made a decision that you have a reason to take the trip. You have a purpose, whether it's to get a gallon of milk, to visit your parents, or to attend a conference. Second, you have a destination you're trying to get to: the grocery store to get milk, Walla Walla to visit your parent's home, or South Barrington, Illinois, for the Church Leadership Conference. Finally, you plot your course: will you speed along the direct route or take the back roads to see the sights?

When it comes to practicing Hitchhiker's Evangelism, these same three steps are critical because they establish the foundation for everything that follows. Before you'll be willing to engage in anything that remotely smacks of evangelism, you have to answer the question, "Why bother?" And "Because the North American church is in trouble" is not a plausible reason, let alone a good one (evangelism isn't a local church membership enhancing practice, it's a kingdom-building practice).

Once you can answer the "Why bother?" question, you need to discern the ultimate destination. Just what does *salvation* mean anyway? Saved from what or saved for what? Frankly, if you don't know what you're offering, you'll probably not practice evangelism because you don't have much to offer.

Finally, before you take one step on a journey to a specific destination, you need to choose a route. To figure out how to get where you're going, you have to know where you're starting from. Your own faith-journey experiences will be the map you use for effective evangelism.

Each chapter in this book concludes with a series of study questions so you can use this book in a small group setting. However, this chapter is a study guide in itself. Each section (Purpose, Destination, and Maps) offers some thoughts for you to consider and questions for you ponder. By the time you finish this chapter, you'll be able to articulate why you will or won't engage in evangelism. You'll have decided for yourself what the Gospel offers. And you'll know how you got to where you are today and perhaps even where you want to go tomorrow!

So, grab a Bible and a pencil, and let's begin this journey together.

Purpose: Why Evangelism?

I was with Bill Easum and a group of mainline pastors some years ago discussing why so many people in the church are hesitant about engaging in evangelism. We bandied about a number of thoughts until finally Easum said, "Until *we* can answer the question, 'What is it about your experience with Jesus that's your neighbors can't live without?' we'll never turn the church around." I think Bill hit the nail squarely on the head. So, let's begin this exercise with his question.

Off the top of your head, what about your experience with Jesus can't your neighbor live without? _____

_____

_____

_____

Hang on to that thought for now. We'll reengage it later on. For the moment, let me offer a couple of reasons why so few Christians in North America practice evangelism.

The cliché answer is simple: the primary reason Christians won't practice evangelism is fear. The thought of sharing your faith can be intimidating. For one, our religion is near and dear to the heart; indeed it's part of our deepest core that molds and shapes us. When we share our faith, we make ourselves vulnerable to ridicule and rejection. For many of us, that risk is just too great, so we protect ourselves by not saying much about what we believe, let alone inviting someone to believe it with us. Others are afraid they don't know enough about the Bible, theology, or the practice of Christianity to share their faith. If we share our faith and someone asks us a question, at best we'll look inept if we can't provide a satisfactory answer. So rather than looking foolish, we keep what we do know to ourselves.

Think of someone you know who isn't a Christian. What keeps you from sharing the Gospel with them?_____

_____

_____

_____

Fear is a potent barrier to sharing our faith. But in my opinion, it isn't the primary excuse. In fact, I believe fear is a distant third on the list of reasons many North American Christians are so reticent to share their faith with Wanderers. I believe the fallout from Kant's arguments is more powerful than fear.

In 1781, Immanuel Kant published his 800-page tome *Critique of Pure Reason.* His work, in part, challenged the tenets of science that proposed that everything was subject to empirical investigation. Kant, who was Christian, argued that religion and truth were not subject to the realm of scientific analysis. In the end, his war of words and his philosophy won out; but in a very real sense, Christianity lost. In effect, instead of elevating the faith above scientific scrutiny, religion was demoted from "ultimate truth" to "just another opinion." Religious beliefs became tantamount to belly buttons—everybody has one, and one belly button is about as good as another.

The notion that all religions are equally true and valid expressions of spirituality has so pervaded our cultural thinking that much of our church has inadvertently embraced the philosophy. We live in a society that endorses both religious toleration and pluralism. Because of this, many Christians have come to the conclusion that they shouldn't "push" their religion on someone else. When that conclusion is translated, it often turns out to mean "I'm not going to *share* my faith with anyone." Why not? Because faith is a personal and a private matter and we shouldn't be messing around with someone's beliefs.

Even though we may disagree that Christianity is just another opinion, we are nonetheless obligated to defend the right for others to believe as they choose even if what they believe isn't truth. Now, I'm certainly not suggesting that people's rights be curtailed, but we've confused the difference between sharing our faith and conversion by the sword. You can't make anyone believe that Jesus is the Son of God, nor should you want to. On the other hand, if you don't share your convictions, the Gospel won't even get a hearing. How can they believe if they have not heard? (Rom. 10:14). As long as we believe that Christianity is just one option among many, we will hesitate to even open a conversation about what we believe and why.

Read John 14:6 and Acts 4:12. How do you think our culture would refute these exclusionary assertions?

> Jesus answered, "I am the way and the truth and the life. No one comes to the Father except through me." (Jn. 14:6)

> Salvation is found in no one else, for there is no other name under heaven given to men by which we must be saved. (Acts 4:12)

_____

_____

_____

_____

Okay, let's leave the issue of why we don't do evangelism for now and turn to why we would (could or should). Yes, I'm aware that I haven't addressed the number one issue for why we don't do evangelism, but we'll get to that, I promise.

People are willing to practice Hitchhiker's Evangelism for a number of reasons. Let's turn to the Bible again and see what it has to offer.

Read Luke 9:26. Church leaders have often used this verse to motivate Christians to do evangelism. In your experience, what kind of motivation does this verse evoke? Is this an effective motivator for you? Why or why not?

If anyone is ashamed of me and my words, the Son of Man will
be ashamed of him when he comes in his glory and in the glory
of the Father and of the holy angels. (Lk. 9:26)

_____

_____

_____

_____

Guilt and shame are powerful motivators that have been used in the
church for generations. However, though these emotional motivators can
bring about positive results, my question is, At what cost? The Bible says
that Hitchhikers—those who are traveling with Jesus along the Way—will
experience a full, meaningful, and joyful life; but guilt and shame rob us
of those promises.

Read Matthew 28:19—20. This is probably the most commonly cited
evangelism passage in the Bible. What is it about these verses that might
motivate Christians to do evangelism? Is this effective motivation in your
life? Why or why not?

Therefore go and make disciples of all nations, baptizing them
in the name of the Father and of the Son and of the Holy Spirit,
and teaching them to obey everything I have commanded you.
And surely I am with you always, to the very end of the age.
(Mt. 28:19—20)

_____

_____

_____

_____

"Jesus commanded it, and that's enough for me" is one of the more
common motivators in the Christian faith. Jesus taught that those who
obeyed him are his friends (Jn. 15:14) and that obedience is a key to his
love (Jn. 14:23—24). However, Jesus hoped to be obeyed because of his
relationship with his followers, not because he was a demanding tyrant
and dictator. The Bible is clear that God isn't pleased with begrudging
obedience. If it's not a heartfelt offering, then it's an unacceptable
offering.

Read John 15:1—11. This may be the second most commonly cited
evangelism passage in the Bible. What about these verses might motivate

Christians to do evangelism? Is this effective motivation in your life? Why or why not?

> I am the true vine, and my Father is the gardener. He cuts off every branch in me that bears no fruit, while every branch that does bear fruit he prunes so that it will be even more fruitful. You are already clean because of the word I have spoken to you. Remain in me, and I will remain in you. No branch can bear fruit by itself; it must remain in the vine. Neither can you bear fruit unless you remain in me. I am the vine; you are the branches. If a man remains in me and I in him, he will bear much fruit; apart from me you can do nothing. If anyone does not remain in me, he is like a branch that is thrown away and withers; such branches are picked up, thrown into the fire and burned. If you remain in me and my words remain in you, ask whatever you wish, and it will be given you. This is to my Father's glory, that you bear much fruit, showing yourselves to be my disciples. As the Father has loved me, so have I loved you. Now remain in my love. If you obey my commands, you will remain in my love, just as I have obeyed my Father's commands and remain in his love. I have told you this so that my joy may be in you and that your joy may be complete. (Jn. 15:1–11)

_____

_____

_____

_____

Experiencing love and joy, experiencing a meaningful relationship with God, having a purpose, and being productive are all common motivations for those who engage in evangelism. Indeed, this is my primary motivation: I want others to enjoy the fulfilling and exciting journey that I share with Jesus. Because of that relationship, I see purpose and meaning in everything that happens around me, both the pleasant and the not so pleasant.

Read Revelation 20:11–15. This passage has historically been used to motivate Christians to engage in evangelism. What about these verses might motivate Christians to do evangelism? Is this effective motivation in your life? Why or why not?

> Then I saw a great white throne and him who was seated on it. Earth and sky fled from his presence, and there was no place

for them. And I saw the dead, great and small, standing before the throne, and books were opened. Another book was opened, which is the book of life. The dead were judged according to what they had done as recorded in the books. The sea gave up the dead that were in it, and death and Hades gave up the dead that were in them, and each person was judged according to what he had done. Then death and Hades were thrown into the lake of fire. The lake of fire is the second death. If anyone's name was not found written in the book of life, he was thrown into the lake of fire. (Rev. 20:11–15)

Fear of hellfire is another common reason why Hitchhikers engage in evangelism. Although sometimes used along with guilt and shame, this fear is felt on behalf of those who may not hear and receive the Gospel and thus be doomed to spend eternity in hell. That's a pretty strong motivation for many who take evangelism seriously. Indeed, for years the hellfire and brimstone sermon was the staple offering of countless preachers and evangelists. Thousands of people responded to the message of salvation from eternal death that only faith in Jesus provided. However, as the North American church has incorporated political correctness into its practice, the threatening nature of the passages that reference hell, Hades, and Sheol have been either diluted, ignored, or avoided. In any event, an enlightened society appears to have little concern about—or belief in—the hell of eternal damnation, flames, and torture.

Which brings us to the next step of our journey: the destination.

Destination: Heaven? Hell? What Is It You're Offering?

You may remember that earlier I claimed to know yet one more reason Hitchhikers don't practice evangelism, a reason more powerful than fear and more pervasive than Kant's arguments. I believe the prevailing reason we don't share our faith with others is because we don't really believe we have anything worth sharing.

When North American Christians are asked, "What is it about your experience with Jesus that your neighbor can't live without?" they tend to be stumped. The notion that I've experienced something my neighbor can't live without seems unrealistic at best and arrogant at worst. I mean, who am I?

Of course, "Who am I?" isn't the question. Ultimately, the question is, "Who is Jesus in relationship to me?" because that's something worth sharing. The relationship I have with Jesus is unique, and yet that kind of relationship is available to my neighbor because of who Jesus is, not because of who I am.

So often when I've seen study questions about what we're offering through our evangelism, the question being asked and answered is, what does someone get by becoming a Christian? In other words, what's in it for me? But that's the wrong question. Jesus isn't Santa Claus with a bag of goodies for us to revel in. Oh sure, we do receive traits, abilities, and gifts when we follow Jesus, but all of them together don't amount to a grain of sand in an oyster. The pearl of great price we receive when we follow Jesus is the answer to the right question, the one I've never seen asked in an evangelism exercise: *Whom* do I get by becoming a Christian?

We have a tendency to fixate on the cost-benefit ratio of the faith, a tendency that the North American church has acquired from our culture. Our nation is built on capitalism. Capitalism depends on consumerism. If we don't consume, society as we know it would grind to a halt. Because we live in a capitalist society, we naturally make our decisions with a "What's in it for me?" attitude. Now, I'm not taking a swing at capitalism here! I'm simply pointing out that it's natural and normal for us to be consumers. So even in the church we inevitably want to know what's the cost and what's in it for us. So, let's take a moment and see what Jesus promised those who chose to follow him.

For each of the following passages, itemize what Jesus promises to those who follow him.

John 5:24

"I tell you the truth, whoever hears my word and believes him who sent me has eternal life and will not be condemned; he has crossed over from death to life."_____

_____

_____

John 14:12–14

"I tell you the truth, anyone who has faith in me will do what I have been doing. He will do even greater things than these, because I am going to the Father. And I will do whatever you ask in my name, so that the Son may bring glory to the Father. You may ask me for anything in my name, and I will do it.

_____

_____

_____

John 17:20–23

"My prayer is not for them alone. I pray also for those who will believe in me through their message, that all of them may be one, Father, just as you are in me and I am in you. May they also be in us so that the world may believe that you have sent me. I have given them the glory that you gave me, that they may be one as we are one: I in them and you in me. May they be brought to complete unity to let the world know that you sent me and have loved them even as you have loved me." _____

_____

_____

John 14:12–14

"I tell you the truth, anyone who has faith in me will do what I have been doing. He will do even greater things than these, because I am going to the Father. And I will do whatever you ask in my name, so that the Son may bring glory to the Father. You may ask me for anything in my name, and I will do it."

_____

_____

John 15:20

"Remember the words I spoke to you: 'No servant is greater than his master.' If they persecuted me, they will persecute you also. If they obeyed my teaching, they will obey yours also."

_____

_____

Matthew 10:16–22

"I am sending you out like sheep among wolves. Therefore be as shrewd as snakes and as innocent as doves. Be on your guard against men; they will hand you over to the local councils and flog you in their synagogues. On my account you will be brought before governors and kings as witnesses to them and to the Gentiles. But when they arrest you, do not worry about what to say or how to say it. At that time you will be given what to say, for it will not be you speaking, but the Spirit of your Father speaking through you. Brother will betray brother to death, and a father his child; children will rebel against their parents and have them put to death. All men will hate you because of me, but he who stands firm to the end will be saved."

_____

_____

_____

Luke 14:25–33

Large crowds were traveling with Jesus, and turning to them he said: "If anyone comes to me and does not hate his father and mother, his wife and children, his brothers and sisters—yes, even his own life—he cannot be my disciple. And anyone who does not carry his cross and follow me cannot be my disciple. Suppose one of you wants to build a tower. Will he not first sit down and estimate the cost to see if he has enough money to complete it? For if he lays the foundation and is not able to finish it, everyone who sees it will ridicule him, saying, 'This fellow began to build and was not able to finish.' Or suppose a king is about to go to war against another king. Will he not first sit down and consider whether he is able with ten thousand men to oppose the one coming against him with twenty thousand? If he is not able, he will send a delegation while the other is still a long way off and will ask for terms of peace. In the same way, any of you who does not give up everything he has cannot be my disciple."

_____

_____

_____

2 Corinthians 1:3–5

Praise be to the God and Father of our Lord Jesus Christ, the Father of compassion and the God of all comfort, who comforts us in all our troubles, so that we can comfort those in any trouble with the comfort we ourselves have received from God. For just as the sufferings of Christ flow over into our lives, so also through Christ our comfort overflows. _____

_____

_____

Read 2 Corinthians 11:23–28 on page 19. Is this the kind of life you thought you signed up for when you became a Christian?

Are they servants of Christ? (I am out of my mind to talk like this.) I am more. I have worked much harder, been in prison more frequently, been flogged more severely, and been exposed to death again and again. Five times I received from the Jews the forty lashes minus one. Three times I was beaten with rods, once I was stoned, three times I was shipwrecked, I spent a night and a day in the open sea, I have been constantly on the move. I have been in danger from rivers, in danger from bandits, in danger from my own countrymen, in danger from Gentiles; in danger in the city, in danger in the country, in danger at sea; and in danger from false brothers. I have labored and toiled and have often gone without sleep; I have known hunger and thirst and have often gone without food; I have been cold and naked. Besides everything else, I face daily the pressure of my concern for all the churches. _____

_____

_____

According to the previous passages, what do we "get" when we choose to follow Jesus?_____

_____

_____

What do you get when you become a Christian? Responsibility, persecution, and trials. But you also get eternal life, which means a full and joyous[6] life both on earth and in heaven. You also receive unity with God, which is an assurance that you can do and experience the things Jesus did, from faithfulness to embracing persecution, from miracles to enduring suffering. When you become a Hitchhiker, you choose a road less traveled—the road Jesus travels. As you pass through the gate that opens the Way to you, Jesus comes and meets you.

Here is the miracle and the mystery of the faith: Jesus comes to each of us uniquely as we live out the purpose we were created for. From this meeting we find our answer to the question, "What is it about your experience with Jesus that your neighbor can't live without?"

I think for many of us in the West this is a new way of understanding our relationship with Jesus. It can seem convoluted or unclear, so let me illustrate with a couple of real-life examples.

Sharon is what some people call a prayer warrior. She regularly spends hours, sometimes even all night, in prayer. She doesn't pray because it's a commandment. She doesn't pray because she's more holy than the rest of us. Sharon prays because she's seen her prayers answered in miraculous ways. Like when she prayed for Brianne.

When Brianne was born, she regularly turned a shade of dark blue for three or four minutes. Her parents took her to their pediatrician who did a complete battery of tests, including x-rays. The films showed Brianne was born with a seriously deformed heart and needed immediate surgery. The doctor made arrangements with the state university's hospital to take over the care, and a surgical consult was scheduled for the following Friday.

I got the call from the parents on Monday and, in turn, let Sharon know. I assured the parents I would come to the hospital for the consultation. On Thursday evening I got a call from Sharon. She'd been praying (all night) and had been given a vision. "Bill, Jesus said the baby's heart is just perfect."

I thanked her for her prayers, and she assured me she'd be continuing to pray. Friday morning came. Of all things, I got lost trying to find the hospital. I arrived several hours late. When I finally found the family, they were just leaving the surgeon's office, and they all had smiles on their faces. "No need for surgery," said the parents.

The hospital had made new films on the baby's heart and, in the exact words of the surgeon, "The baby's heart is just perfect." No deformity. No abnormalities. *Just perfect.* To this date, the pediatrician who took the original films won't give them up because, according to the parents, he says they're his proof that miracles do happen.

I told that story so I could say this: when Jesus came to Sharon, he came as Jesus the healer. For her, that's the Jesus her neighbors can't live without.

Terry is another believer in prayer. Although not the kind of pray-er that Sharon is, Terry spends her day in conversation with God. In the minivan, at her girls' basketball games, in premed classes. Terry's prayers are infinitely practical and applicable to day-to-day life—and she's seen so many answers to her prayers that conversations, even with total strangers, often end up being about the power of prayer.

"I pray about even the simplest things, and God lets us know what to do. My husband and even my children can testify to that," she said. Terry doesn't receive her answers in visions; instead she receives signs. Recently, her husband Kent, who has been underemployed, was offered a job cleaning up the aftermath of hurricane Katrina in New Orleans. The offer came at a time when the family's finances were tight. Terry was inclined to urge him to take the job, but she took the time to pray that God would show them what to do. They had until the end of the week to decide. The very next day, Kent was invited to test for a law enforcement position that he had long wanted. However, with no military experience, no criminal justice training, and no previous invitations even to test, he had concluded he didn't have a hope of entering the field. Two weeks later 112 people tested, and Kent and thirty-four others passed. The law enforcement agency is slated to hire thirty-one new officers. As I write this chapter, no one knows whether or not he'll get one of the positions, but most of us have a hunch he'll be starting classes at the academy sometime soon.

When Jesus came to Terry, he didn't come as a healer, he came as a guide. And that's the Jesus her neighbors can't live without.

I could go on to the tell other stories about how Jesus has come as an encourager, as a protector, and as a companion. Interestingly enough, even here in North America where "real miracles" seem to be somewhat scarce, the experience of Jesus as a healer is by far the most common experience I've encountered. In each of these accounts, the Jesus they've experienced is the Jesus their neighbors can't live without—and they regularly share that Jesus with those they meet. In other words, they practice evangelism in real and tangible ways.

What is it about your experience with Jesus that your neighbors, your community, your world can't live without?_____
_____
_____
_____

In appendix A you'll find a partial list of Jesus' names in the New Testament. It's certainly not exhaustive because, as I suggested earlier, Jesus comes in a unique way to each traveling Hitchhiker. However, if you're having difficulty trying to verbalize the Jesus who comes to you, take some time to reflect on the list and the encounters you have had with Jesus. Because I believe until you can answer that question, you won't really know for sure what you have to offer, or rather, *who* you have to offer.

Your Road Map: Where Are You Starting from?

If I handed you a map, like the one on the next page, and told you to drive to Portland, which way would you go? Would it help if I told you where you are starting from? The answer would be Dayton. Would

it help if I told you which state you were in? There are Daytons in Ohio, Maine, Washington, Idaho, Michigan, California, and in at least a dozen other states. So which direction are you going to take?

In this case, the map is of my grandparents' hometown of Dayton, Oregon, and Portland is north on Highway 223 via Newburg and Tigard.

Our lives are like road maps. If we want to go somewhere, it's helpful knowing where we've been and where we're starting from. When it comes to practicing evangelism while you're hitchhiking with Jesus through life, your past experiences color everything. Allow me to share my evangelism travels.

I was raised in a mainline church. My mom and dad taught Sunday school and were active in the church, and by extension, so was I. By the time I was a young adolescent, I was active in the church youth group and had already experienced Jesus in real and meaningful ways.

It was the late sixties, and the Jesus People Movement was still in full swing. They had a church called River of Life in a nearby town. Our youth group took a field trip there one Sunday. The church was filled with adults in their twenties. At thirteen or so, I was in awe. I'd never been to church where the men didn't wear ties. The women mostly wore dresses that reached to their ankles. They had long flowing hair with flowers pinned in their tresses. The men also had long hair, and many had beards. Instead of ties, they wore strings of beads. The service was charismatic. At the invitation, our whole youth group went forward to receive the gift of tongues. I remember quite distinctly that I was the only one of our group who didn't receive the gift, but I also remember being very moved by the service.

From that moment on, I wanted to share my experience with Jesus with everyone. On Saturdays and Sundays I would join the youth group at ValuMart to hand out Gospel tracts. In junior high, everywhere I went, including to all my classes, I carried several versions of the Bible, a *Strong's Concordance,* a pocket New Testament or two to give away if anyone needed one, and a stack of tracts. I was one of those obnoxious Christian kids, and several of my classmates shackled me with the name Rev, a name I still carry.

My evangelizing methods changed the day I took a Greyhound bus from Seattle to eastern Washington. I was still young, probably fourteen.

When I climbed aboard the bus, it was pretty full. However, one seat was open next to an attractive twenty-something woman. Being a fourteen-year-old male, I decided to sit there. She was reading a paperback, and I was desperate to start a conversation…on several levels. But evangelism was, and still is, one of the primary passions in life, so I mustered up all the courage that an adolescent could, turned to her, cleared my throat, and asked, "Do you know Jesus?"

Let me give you a hint, lest you harbor any doubt in your mind: this is *not* an effective evangelism approach. She stopped reading, looked at me, rolled her eyes, mumbled, "O my God," and shifted in her seat so that I had a view of her back for the rest of the afternoon. It was a long bus ride for both of us.

That's one of the intersections on my personal roadmap. I have others, but that single event changed the way I felt and practiced evangelism for the rest of my life.

What kind of emotions do you feel when you hear the word *evangelism?* _____
_____
_____
_____

What experiences in your past have affected the way you feel about evangelism? _____
_____
_____
_____

Whatever your evangelism history of the past, whether personally experienced or simply witnessed, it has a significant impact on your attitude and your practices today. It seems that most often the resulting emotion is fear. Here is a short list of some fears Christians raise about evangelism:

- Fear of rejection
- Fear of losing friendships
- Fear of losing status
- Fear of losing credibility
- Fear of looking foolish
- Fear of looking like a zealot
- Fear of looking odd

- Fear of offending
- Fear of being persecuted
- Fear of being ridiculed
- Fear of being asked an unanswerable question
- Fear of not knowing what to say
- Fear of being turned down

Circle the fears in the list that you can relate to. On the lines below, add any additional fears of evangelism you may have.

_____
_____
_____

Over the past ten years, have you shared your faith story with someone you knew and had any of your fears come true?

_____
_____
_____

Most of the time when a Hitchhiker experiences fears coming true, it's because the sharing is with a stranger—like my bus ride. On the other hand, as an adult, I can honestly say that none of my fears have ever been realized when I have shared my faith with those I know. Indeed, I've even done the door-to-door, "If you died tonight, do you know for sure you would go to heaven?" kind of evangelism. I can't think of a single time when someone was intentionally rude. (By the way, this isn't one of the evangelism recommendations in this book, so you can release that sharp intake of breath now.) Turns out I'm not unique. Most folks I've spoken with who have practiced Hitchhiker's Evangelism agree that they haven't seen their fears realized either.

Who do you know who isn't a Christian and needs to experience Jesus as you have?

_____
_____
_____

What would it take for you to be comfortable in sharing your faith story with them?

_____
_____
_____

The rest of this book provides a road map to a number of possible Hitchhiker's Evangelism destinations. I'll teach you about painless and fearless ways to introduce your faith to your friends. You'll learn to share your faith at work without getting fired—even if you work in public education. I won't promise that you'll never experience fear or discomfort, but I will promise one thing. If you faithfully take up these tools to share your faith as you travel the Way with Jesus, you will reap a harvest unlike any other.

NOTES

[1]"How Many People Go Regularly to Weekly Religious Services?" *Ontario Consultants on Religious Tolerance,* http://www.religioustolerance.org/rel_rate.htm. (Population and attendance figures based on current United States and Canadian Census data.)

[2]"Number of Unchurched Adults Has Nearly Doubled Since 1991," *The Barna Report,* May 4, 2004, http://www.barna.org/FlexPage.aspx?Page=BarnaUpdate&BarnaUpdateID=163.

[3]Jane Lampman, "New Thirst for Spirituality Being Felt Worldwide," *The Christian Science Monitor* (Nov. 25, 1998). Online at http://www.csmonitor.com/cgi-bin/wit_article.pl?script/98/11/25/112598.feat.feat.17.

[4]Thom S. Rainer, *Surprising Insights from the Unchurched* (Grand Rapids: Zondervan, 2001), 23.

[5]Quoted in "A Vroom with a View," *House2House,* 6 (2002): 34.

[6]Joyous ≠ Happy. We can be profoundly joyous even in extreme suffering, but happiness is fleeting and temporal.

CHAPTER TWO

The Power of Friendship

Two are better than one, because they have a good return for their labor: If they fall down, they can help each other up. But pity those who fall and have no one to help them up! (Eccl. 4:9–10, TNIV)

Quick! Finish this sentence: A friend in need is a _____.

If your answer was "a friend indeed," you're either well versed in clichés or pretty old fashioned. I've been led to believe that Mark Twain quoted that proverb as, "A friend in need is a pain in the neck." Except Twain wasn't big on necks.

Friendship is like roof thatching: it's a vanishing art. Besides, who really has time for friends anymore? Developing friendships is both time consuming and labor intensive. In a society where chasing success and maintaining our independence are marks of a healthy individual, it's a wonder that anyone takes the effort to make friends at all. The popularity of Facebook and MySpace is an indication that we have little desire to get out there and make *new* friends; we can more easily try to resurrect old relationships than risk our time and efforts on building something brand new.

The notion of *friendship evangelism* has been around for a long time in the church. However, the fad never really seemed to take root in North American Christianity. One of the most common confessions

I hear in Christian circles is, "I don't have any unreached friends." In my opinion, these are six of the most heartbreaking words that emerge from a Hitchhiker's mouth. A Christian without an unchurched friend is like a dash of salt in the ocean: it doesn't do anyone any good, and no one even knows it's there. How can a Hitchhiker be a faithful disciple of Jesus and not have any Wanderers or Nomads as friends? Jesus' final command on Earth was to make disciples. And the most effective way to make disciples is to make friends with the unreached. So, why aren't Christians the most friendly people on earth?

Most Christians think we are. I've yet to be in a church that thought it was unfriendly. Indeed, in virtually every church I've ever visited, longtime members will tell me they have the friendliest church in town. The sad reality, though, is that most of these churches are withering on the vine. They've seen few, if any, adult conversions or baptisms in the past decade. But they've got each other. They have their band of congregational friends to hang out with. All the while, their church is dying around them, and they don't understand why.

The answer is obvious. We live in a culture that is by-and-large unchurched. On most Sundays a majority of people in Canada and the United States don't set foot in a church.[1] For many, it doesn't occur to them that church has anything they'd be interested in. Others, however, don't go because they've never been invited by a friend.

Thom Rainer recently wrote that in an extensive survey taken from sea to shining sea across North America, 82 percent of the unreached who were interviewed confessed they would be at least somewhat likely to go to church if a close friend or associate invited them[2]—82 percent. And yet most of our churches in the United States and Canada are in decline. Perhaps we're not as friendly as we'd like to think.

What Keeps Us from Making Friends?

We must have a reason for not making friends with Wanderers and Nomads. Let's be honest! Clearly, we're not as friendly as we claim (or if we are, we're seldom inviting them to come with us to church). For some, making friends with the intent of sharing our faith with them seems manipulative. Some of us are just too busy. And for others of us, we're a bit like Mark Twain: we know friendships can be time consuming and resource expending.

It Feels Like Manipulation

Several years ago my family moved into a planned subdivision that has over 5,000 homes. I was a church planter launching a church in a nearby town, and so I was "too busy" to get to know my neighbors. However, that didn't stop me from encouraging my flock to be busy inviting their friends, relatives, acquaintances, neighbors, coworkers, and everyone else. I personally spent a good bit of time in the area near the church doing the same. But after living in my neighborhood almost two years, the Lord convicted me that I had a nodding acquaintance with only one neighbor and didn't know the names of any of my neighbors. I also knew that in my section of the nation there was about a 97 percent chance that each of my neighbors were unchurched. I decided it was well past time to do something. So I started praying for opportunities to meet them and began to make appearances at timely intervals to meet those who lived around me.

I met Carl,[3] the neighbor directly across the street from me and started praying for opportunities to get to know him well enough to discover his faith receptivity—it's not generally helpful to meet and greet your neighbors for the first time saying, "So, do you know Jesus?" I knew I had to earn the right to share my faith, so I began to discover inroads to become Carl's friend.

Whenever I teach about practicing Hitchhiker's Evangelism and making friends with the hope of sharing our faith, someone will object and claim it's manipulative to make friends when we have a premeditated objective of sharing our faith. I could not disagree strongly enough. It would be manipulative to weasel into a relationship in the guise of friendship to evangelize a newfound "friend." It is quite another thing to become a friend and be intentional about sharing the Gospel. To illustrate, let me continue with my story about Carl.

I knew that there was a really good chance that Carl was unchurched, so I put a good bit of effort into getting to know him as spring came to an end and the Northwest summer, such as it is, began. Our relationship started with sincere compliments about his landscaping and chitchat about the weather. Over time our conversation moved toward more intimate subjects like what color to repaint my house and whether the postman would be on time. In other words, our relationship remained pretty superficial for quite some time. However, by the end of the summer we discovered we had a mutual interest—we were both committed Christians.

Now, if my sole intention had been to convert Carl, our friendship would have waned as soon as I discovered he was no longer a new prospect for the kingdom. Instead, my intent was to make a friend with whom I could share my faith, something I succeeded at. Whether Carl was a fellow Hitchhiker or not was irrelevant to my friendship. Yes, I was intentionally hoping to share my faith with an unbeliever, but that had no bearing on whether or not I was going to intentionally befriend my neighbor. If Carl had been a Wanderer, yes, at the right time I would have shared my faith. But if he had not been receptive to my faith, I would not have ceased being his friend and started looking for a new "mark" for my scam (and it would be a scam if I only poised as a friend to share the faith). Instead, if Carl had not been a Christian, I would have continued to be his friend and perhaps one day he would have become more receptive. Or perhaps not. In any event, I planned on continuing to be a neighbor and a friend. Ultimately, what I discovered was that I do have someone with whom I can share my faith, a friend who now shares my faith journey.

I find it interesting that in business, a wide variety of opportunities are created through clubs and networking organizations to bring prospective clients and business ventures together. No one seems to regard these organizations as manipulative even though their express purpose is to further business opportunities for their members. Instead, they consider themselves a service to the community.

Friendships are more than a commercial commodity, and they're more important. In fact, they are a human necessity. Friends normally share their time, their knowledge, and even their wealth with each other. Sharing our faith with a friend isn't an act of subterfuge; it's an act of friendship.

But I Don't Have Time for Another Friend

Friend making is time consuming. Friendships can be a drain on our resources, especially on our time. Back in the fifties and sixties, scientists predicted that within a decade or two the development of labor-saving devices and automation in manufacturing and agriculture would lead us to the promised land of twenty- to thirty-hour workweeks. We'd have so much leisure time that we wouldn't know what to do. Well, it turns out that we're working more hours per week than we were back then and have significantly less time for ourselves, let alone others. It's no wonder one of the great excuses for not being an intentional friend maker is that we don't have time.

The fact is, if we're too busy to have friends, then we're just *too busy* and need to do something about it. God did not create us to live solitary lives with little or no significant social interaction. People need community, and community extends beyond the garage doors. The New Testament provides no examples of hermits or isolated families. Even the lepers came together and lived in "colonies." Community is the norm for Christians and for all other segments of humanity.

So, you may be wondering, isn't the community in our churches enough? Turning again to the New Testament, we do find an "inner community" of like-minded believers. Still, Jesus, the disciples, Paul, and virtually every other New Testament character we meet spent significant time with unbelievers. Once again, faithfulness to the Great Commission demands rubbing shoulders with Wanderers.

But what about the time issue? How can we fit a new friend into our already busy schedule? Although we'll get to prioritizing time later on in this chapter, let me introduce a few brief observations. Though a dinner party takes significant preparation, you're probably going to make something to eat this evening anyway. Consider inviting your neighbor to dinner—nothing fancy, just dinner. If you're a moviegoer, invite a potential friend along with you the next time you go. If you were planning on taking your family, invite them anyway; and if they have a family, invite them to bring theirs. If you're a video viewer, next time you check out the newest release, call that new coworker to join you. Maybe they can bring the microwave popcorn. You get the idea. To build a casual relationship into a new friendship, you can add an acquaintance to almost any activity you were planning. It doesn't have to be time intensive, just time intentional.

I Don't Have the Energy for Another Friend

At times Mark Twain's comment about friends resonates with my heart. When I lived in a small town in the Midwest, I got to be known as one of the techie gurus. I knew enough about software and hardware to be slightly less than dangerous. I tended to know what was current in the computer world. On the other hand, my neighbor Paul was a computer neophyte. So as we became friends, I naturally became one of his on-site tech support persons. Let me be quick to say that Paul never abused my friendship, but I must also confess that being his friend wasn't always convenient. You see, one of the perks of friendship is that you allow others to have a claim on your life. When Paul got stuck with some tech question—though he often tried to solve the issue himself—he called me when he needed to be bailed out. Sometimes I could solve his problem over the phone. However, most of the time it was easier to meet at his office and walk him through the issue. It seemed Paul seldom needed my help when it was convenient. On the other hand, if he had to wait on me to experience an opportune moment, he'd still be waiting. The claims on friendships are almost never convenient.

I suppose meeting people's needs wasn't convenient for Jesus either. Seems to me, he and the boys were looking forward to a weekend off when he told the disciples, "Come with me by yourselves to a quiet place and get some rest" (Mk. 6:31). But someone saw them leave and followed them, bringing the crowd in tow, and the guys didn't get a break. Convenient? No. But it's what we do—or at least, what we're supposed to be all about.

Friends in need can be a pain in the neck indeed. At the very minimum, they can be inconvenient. But Jesus didn't call us to a Gospel of convenience; the Gospel that calls us can be *very* inconvenient. Nowhere in the New Testament are we promised lives of convenience and prosperity, contrary to the distortions I've heard from many of the popular preachers. (In fact, I'm still waiting for someone to identify the New Testament follower of Jesus who was the model for the health and wealth doctrine.) Instead, Jesus promised his followers hardships, heartaches, and headaches. Seems to me, though, the inconveniences that a friendship can pose are miniscule compared to the claims of the Great Commission on the life of a Hitchhiker.

Why Be Friends?

We've covered the key excuses for why we don't make the effort to develop new friendships and, with just a little bit of luck, I've even begun to convince you that you may have some good reasons to reach out and make a new friend or two. But I believe friendship making is important enough to warrant a few words specifically about why we should want to start making new friends.

It's Creation's Way

In the very beginning God said that it wasn't good for us to be alone. The first commandment God gave us as humans was to be fruitful and multiply—in other words, to build a wider community. When I look throughout scripture, I note that all that multiplying didn't seem to create a thousand islands of solitude but rather nations of communities. Friendships are the foundation of those communities. People naturally gravitate to each other. Now, for those who are musing, "I thought marriage and family were the foundation of our society," let me point out that successful families are built on the principles of friendship. Indeed, I worry about couples who aren't friends above all else. God created us for community.

Friendships may be inconvenient at times, but many times *we* are the friend in need. Friendships provide a measure of safety and security in an uncertain world. Blood may well be thicker than water, but good friends are the ones you can count on when the chips are down. They're the ones with the pickups when it's time to move, they're the dog-sitters when you go out of town, and the ones who will cry with you over spilt milk when everyone else tells you to suck it up and be strong. They depend on you, and you depend on them. That's how life works.

It's a Jesus Thing

I could name a dozen other good reasons for getting out there and making new friends, but the most important one for the Christian is that it's a Jesus thing that the rest of the world probably won't fully understand. The parting words of Jesus to his disciples was to get out there and win one for the Gipper—or words to that effect. He said something about how we should "make disciples" (Mt. 28:19) and be my witnesses in your neighborhood, community, and beyond (Acts 1:8). That's the Great Commission, and friendship-building is probably the most effective way to fulfill it.

Virtually every poll that asks how an individual became a Christian reveals that over 90 percent of us were invited either to church or into a relationship with Jesus by a close friend or a relative. As effective as the Billy Graham crusades, television and radio preaching, Gideon Bibles, and door-to-door evangelism campaigns may be, even when combined they don't compare to the effectiveness of one friend inviting another to join the faith journey. The fact is, friendship evangelism works! It works to such a degree that if American Christians ever got serious about sharing their faith with their neighbors we'd fill all our church buildings beyond capacity, not unlike the first Pentecost Sunday when 3,000 people showed up for the first church service (read Acts 2 in the New Testament for more details). The most effective way to reach a Wanderer is to build a significant friendship with them as you travel the Way and share your faith as one friend to another.

Whenever we touch a life for Jesus that is outside the walls of the church (that is, someone not born into the church), Christianity increases its span of influence. According to sociologists, most of us have a significant relationship network of just over six people. Indeed, some suggest we may have as many as nine people with whom we have significant influence. If

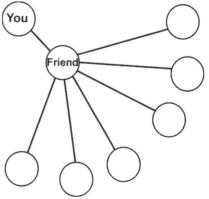

we befriend a single unchurched person who is outside of our regular network, the Gospel has the opportunity to reach at least six additional people, most of whom will also be unchurched.

The implications of this for the sake of the kingdom and for the church is significant. With 82 percent of the unchurched population admitting they would at least be somewhat likely to attend a church if a close friend invited them, imagine the impact if even half of us intentionally made an unchurched friend this year and shared our faith with them.

A Word for You Guys

In our culture, women somehow appear to be more adept at significant friendships than us guys. Oh sure, in some career fields guys still have close friends—the military, police, and firefighters come to mind. But for many, if not most of us, we seem to have grown out of close friendships with the guys when we left high school or the frat house. Perhaps this occurs because we're a nation where independence is championed, and interdependence is, well, looked upon as a weakness.

Except, having done my own informal and rather unscientific study, I've discovered a bunch of us guys privately pine for a couple of guys we could be friends with. You know, the kind of guys you can really be honest with. Guys who shoot straight and don't laugh when you confess you couldn't tell a carburetor from an injector. Guys for whom you'd be willing to go to bat, and who would go to bat for you in the crunch. Not just a round of golf kind of friend, but the kind of guy who'd come looking for you and drive you home when your whole world falls apart at four in the morning. *That* kind of friend.

Guys, if you don't have that kind of friendship, let me invite you to find a way to make a couple of friends like that. We're missing something when we don't have friends of the same gender. Some things only guys really understand. Society has done its best to tame us and curtail our masculinity, but the world still needs knights in shining armor, gallant princes, and courageous gentlemen. Because most guys in our culture don't have a band of brothers to depend on—and too few of us have had shining, gallant, courageous role models—you might as well begin building such a network with an unchurched friend. It'll do you both good. I know it did for me and for the guys with whom I've been intentionally building relationships over the past few years.

Prioritizing Time for Friendships

I hope by now I've convinced you that making friends is important, not only for the kingdom of God but for you personally as well. I've dealt with a couple of the objections people typically quote to justify not making friends, but we honestly still seem to have less time than we need to do those things we know we ought to do.

Everyone has the same amount of time each day; however, we all probably know people who seem to be able to pack their day just right so that they get more out of it than we do. We often wonder what their secret is to getting all that "stuff" accomplished. But they really have no secret. They've just learned how to prioritize their time differently and more adequately.

The end of this chapter offers a couple of questions to help you consider what your current priorities are. This could be a revealing exercise as you think about how to fit a new friend into your schedule. But first, let's explore some ways to add a new friendship to your life.

Friendships on the Run

I introduced the first suggestion earlier in this chapter. We assume we will have to set aside time from our routine to fit in a new friendship, but this needn't be the case. Time is limited, but we have to eat dinner anyway. You might as well invite a new friend to share it with you. Sure, the house may not be spotless, but many of us have a tendency to overemphasize appearances anyway. Though it might be nice to throw a dinner party complete with decorations and fine dining, many of us don't have time to put one together anytime soon. Besides, for some, dinner parties tend to be less relaxed and may actually be a barrier to more casual and intimate conversation. As much as my wife likes setting a beautiful table, complete with the appropriate silver settings and all our plates for soup, salad, entrée, bread, and dessert, we've found this to be not only time consuming and cumbersome in preparation and cleanup, it has confused a number of our friends. We began to take note when more than one dinner guest confessed their uncertainty about whether or not they were using the "right" fork or knife.

Lately, we've chosen to save the etiquette lessons for our kids and opt for hosting simpler gatherings that negate the risk of serving undue embarrassment to our friends. It's not that we've completely given up on the formal dinner option, only that we find ourselves in a place where simpler is better and more than adequate. On the other hand, we have friends who thrive well on hosting formal dinner parties; and we ourselves always enjoy being invited to join them! As new friendships unfold, it can take time to get to know one another at our various comfort levels. Simplicity is an important key that works both to our advantage and for the benefit of our budding relationships.

The opportunities to include new friends in our daily lives are almost limitless. Invite someone to go shopping or to garage sales with you. Invite your neighbor to watch the high school football game with you. Go look at Christmas lights or watch fireworks together. Request the honor of their presence at the next library book reading or speaker event. Take your morning walk, jog, or bike ride with a new acquaintance. You get the picture. From movies to golf, adult education at the junior college to a fun class at the senior center, you can find plenty of ways to expand your network of friends.

Doing the Important before the Urgent

One of those popular e-mails that made the circuit recently I found particularly germane to this discussion. During the first class period in a college physics course, a wise professor produced a four-liter glass jar filled to the brim with golf balls. He set the jar on the lab table before him and asked the students, "Is this jar full?" The students as one said, "Yes." Reaching below the table, the professor revealed a beaker with ball bearings in it. He began to pour the bearings into the jar, shaking it until the spaces between the golf balls were filled. He then asked the class again, "Is this jar full?" With a little less certainty the students responded, "Yes." The professor reached beneath the table and produced a beaker with sand in it, and he proceeded to add the contents into the jar until the sand filled the jar to the brim. Turing to the class he asked again, "Is this jar full?" This time the students were certain. "Yes!" A third time the professor revealed a beaker, this time filled with water. The class groaned as he poured the contents into the jar.

Turning to the class the professor said, "The golf balls are those important tasks in your life that each of you here is uniquely equipped to handle. The bearings are lesser important chores that need to be accomplished to keep your life running smoothly, but will divide your attention from the important tasks. The sand is the gritty day-to-day urgent demands of life that will distract you from your purpose. And the water is the details that will attempt to fill your life if you let them. Attend to the important first; or the chores, the urgent, and the details will crowd out and drown your dreams."

Put It on the Calendar

Of course, the important will never get done if you don't make it "real." I carry a PDA that I only half jokingly say is my life. If an appointment isn't in my PDA, it doesn't exist—at least not for me. It's not "real" until it's on my calendar. For the important to get accomplished, it has to make it onto your calendar; and you have to follow through with those pesky details. For instance, putting your neighbor on the calendar for dessert will not make it happen. You have to actually invite them. You have to remember to ask if they have any allergies or food restrictions before shopping for your Friday evening event. If you're like my wife and me, you more than likely will have to hit the grocery store for ingredients or something to warm up and put on the dessert plates. Get it all down on the calendar step-by-step! Before you know it, you'll have loads of new unchurched friends. And if you have just one unchurched friend, you already have more than the vast majority of Christians.

I'm not sure I need to comment further. The exercises at the end of the chapter will help you decide what's important and what's urgent. But let's take this another step.

Getting ENOF

Okay, you're convinced. You want to make a difference in the kingdom of God, and you're ready to make a couple of friends in the unreached sector. But you don't know any unchurched people. Where do you find them?

This is an important question that I'm asked all the time. Recently, I helped launch a network of house churches. These home fellowships focused on reaching the unchurched. For these people one of the biggest impediments was the question about where to find an unchurched person. I had to smile in wonderment in the Pacific Northwest when I heard this concern, because out there as many as 93 percent of the population was functionally unchurched. That means only one out of ten people wasn't a prospect for a new unchurched friend. And yet, "I don't know any unchurched people" remained the most common refrain I heard.

We all need ENOF—an **E**xpanding **N**etwork **O**f **F**riends. Finding unchurched and unreached friends isn't nearly as difficult as it may seem. In fact, you are probably already acquainted with half a dozen without realizing it. This is such an important topic that I've devoted a whole chapter to it later on, but let me get the wheels turning here by getting you to think through a couple of questions.

- Do you know all your immediate neighbors? Do they all go to church?
- Is your doctor a Christian?
- How about your dentist?

- Your mechanic?
- Think through your workplace. Is everyone a Christian there?

The list could go on and on, but this gives you a start. If you're ready to jump in, make the chapter on ENOF the next one you read (but not until you've worked through the study questions at the end of this chapter).

Friend Making 101

In the beginning of this chapter I used the analogy of roof thatching for friend making. Both seem to be dying arts (just try to find a roof thatcher in your Yellow Pages!). As we head for the homestretch in this chapter, let's review some of the friend-making skills we all need. This will probably be a review for you, but it may be a good review because most of us are pretty rusty at getting out of the house to make a new friend.

Barbecue First

Mark Mittelberg recounts a story of one of his early attempts to reach a new neighbor for Christ. Mark's faith was bubbling overboard. He barely knew the new residents' names when he extended an invitation to them for a church event. You may have guessed that their response was less than positive. Mark says he kicked himself, and from then on applied the axiom "Barbecue First."[4]

I've taken Mark's advice when it comes to his axiom. One of the first things my wife and I consistently do to expand our network of friends is invite neighbors and other potential friends to a barbecue at our home. We have a grill on our back deck and love to entertain by cooking out between rain squalls in the Seattle summer. The "barbecue first" rule is a reminder that to make friends with anyone, let alone someone who is unchurched, we have to invest both time and proximity. During the winter, dinner may need to be chili or a pineapple chicken, but invite them to *whatever* your "barbecue" may be, whether it's spaghetti and a video or fondue and wine.

Remember Carl? It took me nearly all summer to find out that Carl was a Christian. Don't rush friendship making. Remember you're creating a lifelong relationship, not a one-night stand.

Have Something in Common

Another rule, or reality, of friendship making is that not everyone is going to be your friend. Not everybody is going to click with you, let alone like you and want to be your friend. As a pastor, this is one of the most difficult truths I have had to learn. Like most people, I want to be liked. I have often been devastated by discovering someone in my parish doesn't think I'm God's gift to the congregation. On the other hand, I know people I'd rather not spend an afternoon with either.

The same holds true when being intentional about making friends in the unchurched world. God hasn't called me to reach every single person in my neighborhood—which doesn't let me off the hook from trying—but the reality is, some people like me and some don't. Those who don't will probably never be receptive to my faith story. That's okay! God has someone else for them (although that leaves open the whole question of whether or not *they'll* be faithful to God's bidding to build that relationship).

Building friendships means sharing common interests. Carl and I both enjoy taking walks and discussing biblical metaphors. And of course, he picks my brain about computers, and I pick his brain for gardening tips. Friendships are built on common interests.

On the other hand, if you're going to build a friendship, you may have to create a common interest. In the chapter about vendors you'll be introduced to Jeff, an unchurched friend of mine. I mention Jeff here because although he and I have a common interest in computers, he makes his living at it but it's not his calling. In other words, he'd just as rather not spend our time together chatting bits and bytes. Jeff does, however, love to bicycle. I didn't even own a bike, but he loves it so much that I told him I was thinking about getting a bike so we could ride together. He was so excited that I would want to spend time together riding that he gave me a really nice racing bicycle. In Jeff's case, I developed a common interest with him.

Friendships are based on lots of things, but you've got to have something in common to make it work. If you don't click with your unchurched neighbor and you have nothing besides a property line in common, don't worry about it. You're not relieved of being a great neighbor, but you don't have to be friends. On the other hand, if your other neighbor seems like a nice person you'd like to get to know better, spend time learning what you have in common. If you don't find something obvious, consider building a common interest.

Becoming a Friend

Once you've launched into friendship building, the next step is to actually become a friend. Getting to know your unchurched neighbor is a good first step. Spending time in regular proximity sharing common interests will lay a foundation. But moving from the acquaintance level to friendship takes multiple acts of intentionality. You need to be available, transparent, and forbearing.

Be Available

Here Mark Twain's words come to bear on our reality. When you move from being an acquaintance to a friend, you're choosing to make yourself available. Good friends are there through thick and thin. That means when the going gets tough, friends get called on. Long before I had a pickup, I was one of the first people who got called to help friends move. Why? Because I made sure I was available for my friends. Do I like helping people move? I don't even like moving myself, let alone being semi-responsible for someone else's household treasures. But that's one of the costs of being a friend.

A friend will be more interested in your availability than they will be your ability. In the movie *Crocodile Dundee,* Mick Dundee explains that the people of Walkabout Creek don't need psychoanalysis, because they have friends to talk to. Truth be told, many people in therapy could save themselves a small fortune if they just had a good friend who was available to listen to them. Being available is probably the most important task of a lasting friendship.

Be Transparent

If friends are anything, they're real. Over time, Carl has come to know me better and better. He doesn't yet know *all* my warts and scars, but he knows about a bunch of them because as I've gotten to know him, I've learned I can trust him with my heart. Transparency is an important ingredient in any friendship.

To be a friend, you will have to prove yourself trustworthy. That means when your newfound friend is ready to open up to you, you will be (1) available, (2) ready to listen, and (3) able to keep their confidence confidential. Twelve Step participants remember and affirm at each meeting that "who you see here, what you hear here, when you leave here, let it stay here." That means when your friend gets transparent, it stays with you. Not you and your spouse. Not you and their spouse. Between you and them.[5] You should also expect the same from them, and indeed, you may have to be the one to open the doors of transparency.

Once again, be careful about when you share your deepest wounds or secrets. The barbecue first rule applies here as well, except you may want to expand that to "a bunch of barbecues" before you share. When you do begin to share, don't unload every detail of your whole sordid past (if you have a sordid past!). A little bit can go a long way. When being transparent, taking baby steps is the rule. Share a little bit here and a little bit there, slowly opening your heart's hurts and desires. Over time, as you share, you will probably, little by little, be the recipient of their heart and hurts. This is an incredible gift, so handle it as the precious treasure it is.

Be Forgiving

Finally, contrary to the classic movie *Love Story,* your really do need to say you're sorry. You need to be ready to forgive if you're going to build a lasting friendship. Unfortunately, people are humans who err. I have ADHD (Attention Deficit Hyperactivity Disorder), which means I didn't develop some of the social filters most people get while they are growing up. This results in my inadvertently stepping on people's toes and hurting their feelings far too often. I don't mean to be blunt, and I don't generally think of myself as being blunt, but apparently I am. If someone is going to be my friend, they end up having to come to terms with me. I have no excuse for my actions, but the reality is that if you're around me long enough, I'll probably open mouth and insert foot. And I'll almost certainly need your forgiveness.

Forgiveness is a mark of a true friend. We all say and do dumb things, so we all need to be forgiven. When you spend time with an unreached friend, don't expect them to live by anything that looks like a Christian's moral or ethical standard. They're not Christians, so don't expect Christian behavior. Among other things, they may cancel without calling or totally forget you were supposed to get together. They may not consider your scheduled time together to be as important as you do. Some of your Wanderer friends may be a little rough around the edges (of course, so are we sometimes). This all means you're going to have to forgive them now and again. And they'll have to forgive you, too, because you're going to mess up now and again as well.

However, a narrow line separates forgiving and enabling. Having ADHD is not an excuse for poor behavior. My friends should expect to be treated with dignity, honesty, respect, and kindness. When I say or do something hurtful, I need to be confronted; and my behavior needs to change. I'm glad to say I don't tend to make the same mistakes over and over. The same kind of mistakes, sure, but I am a fast learner. I'm getting better with each incident. On the other hand, I know people who expect to be forgiven and move their relationships back to normal even though they make the same mistakes over and over and over again.

Forgiving doesn't mean a lack of accountability. If I repeatedly said the same thoughtless comment about someone, accountability requires that the relationship would need to be terminated, even if I said I was sorry each time. Unless behavior changes, confession isn't repentance; and nothing will change. In no way does forgiveness suggest relinquishing accountability. None of us deserves—or is expected to bear the brunt of—someone's denigration, meanness, hostility, or other hurtfulness.

Conclusion

I hope as you've read this chapter you've been convicted about making friends with your unchurched neighbors. And I hope that the suggestions I've offered will help you in your quest to become a new friend. On the next pages are study questions for this chapter. Take some time to go over them. Discuss them in a small group or with one of your current friends. When you've finished, you'll have a plan of action for getting out there and being faithful to the Great Commission in your neighborhood.

By the Way Reflections

1. Pull out your calendar. On what two tasks or chores have you spent the most time over the past two months? How does that make you feel: satisfied, justified, horrified, embarrassed, happy, sad?
2. How much time have you spent with an unchurched person? With unchurched people?
3. Whom do you know that you could "get to know better" over the next two months? List at least three people. (Note: you may not yet know their names, just where they live, what they do, or where you usually see them.)
4. List five ways you can use to get to know at least one of the above-listed people better. Make sure you include appropriate ways both to meet them more formally and to move past casual introductions.
5. Grab your calendar again, and schedule a deadline for meeting and doing something with (or for) this person.

NOTES

[1]According to religioustolerance.org, 43 percent of people in the United States and 20 percent of Canadians say they go to church weekly, though how honest people are when surveyed about church attendance is up for debate. See http://www.religioustolerance.org/rel_rate.htm.

[2]Thom S. Rainer, *The Unchurched Next Door* (Grand Rapids: Zondervan, 2003), 24.

[3]Not his real name.

[4]Bill Hybels and Mark Mittelberg, *Becoming a Contagious Christian* (Grand Rapids: Zondervan, 1994), 97–98.

[5]Of course, exceptions occur. If your friend shares they're going to do something illegal, are a danger to themselves or someone else, you have no choice but to do something about it.

CHAPTER THREE

Vendors

Choose Whom You Use

*Be wise in the way you act toward outsiders; make the most of
every opportunity. Let your conversation be always full of grace,
seasoned with salt, so that you may know how to answer everyone.
(Col. 4:5–6)*

For a brief period of my adult life, I lived in a small, rural Midwestern
community about four-and-a-half miles just east of nowhere. In that little
hamlet I learned a couple of very important lessons. First, I'm not much
of a rural person. I need to live where I can't walk the town's perimeter
in fifteen minutes or less. Second, I'm *really* not a rural person. I need
to live somewhere larger than a town where everyone knows me, greets
me, and waves at me when they drive by (and expects me to wave back
every time, lest they feel slighted). Third, and perhaps most importantly,
I'm not a rural person (did I just say that?). I discovered I need to be able
to go shopping and have more than three choices of canned vegetables
or lunch meat.

They say you don't know what you have until you've lost it. When I
lived in this rural community, I discovered that freedom can be defined
as having multiple choices. I yearned for the freedom to choose between
more than just caffeinated or decaffeinated coffee. I pined for the freedom
to be overwhelmed while trying to choose which breakfast cereal I want.
I missed the freedom to choose which vendors I wanted to patronize.

Vendors tend to be the invisible people in our lives (but they start getting really visible when you don't have many choices). From the greeters at Wal-Mart to the grocery store clerk at the A&P, vendors are those people who give their lives to service by providing us multiple choices.

Most of us don't give the vendors, that is the people who provide us with choices, a second thought. If we need milk, we go to the local grocer. If we need staples, we go to the office supply store. If we need our hair cut, we go to our stylist (or barber, as the case may be). In each of these cases, we make a choice about which vendor we're going to patronize.

. In the life of a Christian, though, there's more to choice than merely deciding between Captain Crunch or Shredded Wheat, Wal-Mart or our local hardware store. Whenever we make one of these choices, we employ the opportunity to make a difference in the name of Christ.

Beggars Can't Be Choosers, but Christians Should Be

Ideally, every decision a Christian makes is made prayerfully. This is never more true than when choosing a vendor. Whether you're choosing where to buy your groceries or buying a new car, the decision of which vendor you choose can have eternal consequences—so choose carefully.

Making Eternal Choices

I've been accused of preferring the company of the "pagans" over the "righteous." To the charge, I plead guilty. The fact is, as much as I love spending time with the One-Anothers, I enjoy even more being in the presence of the Everyone-Elses.

The Bible contains over forty one-another commands, instructions for how we treat others.[1] Now if you were raised in the church, you probably got the party line that the one-another commands in the Bible applied to how we were supposed to treat everybody. To be fair, when Jesus said, "Love one another" he was teaching us that our love is to reach out beyond ourselves and into the whole world. We *are* supposed to love our "neighbor" as ourselves and to love and pray for our "enemies." Still, the application of the one-another commands is actually reserved for the family of faith. For instance, the scriptures say we should "confess your sins to one another" (Jas. 5:16, NRSV) and "submit to one another" (Eph. 5:21); however, doing either with the unchurched would be inappropriate. Some have argued that the use of "one another" is simply generic and used interchangeably, but a glance at 1 Thessalonians suggests otherwise.

In 1 Thessalonians 5:15 and 3:12 Paul clearly makes a delineation between the two: "Make sure that nobody pays back wrong for wrong, but always try to be kind to each other and to everyone else." Yes, we are to be kind to everyone, but note that he makes a distinction that is not accidental.

I love the One-Anothers. I do my best to be an encourager to those in the church. However, truth be known, we already have an eternity to spend together down the line. On the other hand, Paul asks in his letter to the Romans how people will hear about the good news if someone doesn't tell them (10:14). Jesus told the parable of the good shepherd who leaves the ninety-nine to go find the wandering lamb (Luke 15). And so, I do my best to spend as much time with the Everyone-Elses as I can.

This choice involves a paradox, however. Many Christians in the marketplace expect their fellow Christians to patronize their businesses. We do have a number of good reasons to support one another in the marketplace, and for most churched people this is probably the best option of all. For these the question should be, "Who *needs* my business?" However, those interested enough in faith sharing to read this book have in some way expressed a desire to share their faith in a meaningful way. For us, the question, "Who needs my business?" is an irrelevant query. Instead, we have one primary question to answer: "Who can I most effectively share my faith with?"

Now, let me be clear. This is not an invitation to stop shopping at your local Bible bookstore to save fifty cents by shopping at Wal-Mart because you might be able to share your faith with a clerk. As you will see in a moment, faith sharing depends on building relationships. If you're willing to make the effort to build a relationship with a particular clerk at Wal-Mart, then by all means, do so. But for most of us, a super-department-store experience is less about the people and more about the shopping—especially bargain shopping (gotta save that quarter). If your purpose is shopping, visit your local Christian vendor to make your purchases—loving one another demands it. On the other hand, if your desire is to share your faith, you'll need to go somewhere to build relationships with Wanderers. Remember, the choice you make really does have eternal consequences.

Where Would Jesus Shop?

The WWJD craze of the nineties nearly trivialized the basic behavioral question every Christian must ask: Just what *is it* that Jesus would do? If he's the model for faith and behavior, we must never lose sight of that question. So when I pose the question, "Where would Jesus shop?" I'm being neither irreverent nor frivolous. Although I believe Jesus would generally have done his shopping in the unchurched marketplace, that still leaves us with a huge question: "Would Jesus patronize a locally owned family business or a megamart?"

The watchwords for the church in the United States and Canada in the twentieth century were *social action*. Although the church has always had a hand in relieving suffering and trying to make the world a better place to live, much of the modern church has shifted its focus from the personal touch to social activism. Christians have come to believe that by getting involved in lobbying and politicking they can affect wholesale social changes. Indeed, the church has managed to make a few positive social inroads, but for every step forward we take politically, we seem to lose face in the public forum. In the last century, the church "won" Prohibition, but ultimately it eroded the public's confidence in the triumph of godliness. Forty years ago, a portion of the church supported civil liberties and equality for people of color, while other churches supported continued oppression and the status quo. In what should have been an open-and-shut case for Hitchhikers, the church's deep divisions became apparent to a watching and bewildered nation.

For decades the church has had a hand in trying to influence the wider society from the top down through a variety of legislative avenues. But let's be honest, we've either lost, or are losing, nearly every battle we take up in the public forum: abortion, homosexuality, gambling, prayer in school, the public display of the Ten Commandments, even displaying nativity scenes on public property or wishing customers "Merry Christmas."

In some communities, especially in rural towns and suburbia, a distinct anti-megamart mentality has galvanized local churches to organize in an attempt to restrict or ban corporate America from impinging. Indeed, because these corporations have the resources to buy in volume, they can sell their wares at a discounted price. In fact, they regularly will sell popular items at a loss to drive traffic into their stores (these are called loss leaders and virtually every grocery store chain in the United States practices this marketing ploy). Because of these practices, locally owned shops cannot compete—especially in rural areas where transportation costs are an issue. Local churches and civic groups often join together to protect the resident businesses that depend on the larger community's patronage. Hitchhikers and Wanderers alike argue both sides of the fence.

But let's not lose sight of the ultimate reason for choosing where we shop: Can our patronage make an eternal difference? In many regions, patronizing a locally owned business increases our influence well beyond what our dollars can buy; however, the point of shopping locally is neither to manipulate nor to create a sense of indebtedness to share our faith. On the other hand, fostering an atmosphere of goodwill can be helpful in our bridge-making and relationship-building attempts—the twin keys to effective faith sharing.

So, where would Jesus shop? I'm convinced Jesus would shop (and probably shopped) wherever he could have an opportunity to make an eternal difference—whether that was a local business or a megamart. Wherever souls had as yet to be reached, there we'd find Jesus striking up a conversation.

Familiarity Breeds Opportunity

I have a couple of hitchhiking friends who have the gift of evangelism. These folks can get into an evangelistic, share-Jesus kind of conversation with a complete stranger in a grocery story checkout line and do so without offending anyone. Sometimes I really envy them. But those moments of envy are infrequent and blessedly brief. I've done the knock-on-the-door "If you died tonight" kind of evangelism, and I was relatively successful at it. However, for every individual I led to Jesus, I may have inoculated ten others from the faith. I suspect I'm going to be held accountable for those I alienated.

You see, instead of sharing my heart or my life with these folks, I was sharing a plan. These people didn't know me, and most of them, frankly, didn't want to know me. Especially not after I'd interrupted their lives with a sales pitch about Jesus.

Someone once said that no one cares how much you know until they know how much you care. This is never more true than when sharing our faith. I often speak about earning the right to share faith with someone. It's a matter of getting a hearing. I'm more liable to be heard by someone who knows me and who knows how I live my life than by someone who doesn't, at least assuming my life isn't an embarrassment to the Gospel.

Which is why it's so important to be intentional about where we shop—familiarity breeds opportunity.

Quick—what's the name of your favorite grocery store checker where you shop? And is he or she married? Do you even have a favorite grocery store checker?

If you live in a small town, you might actually have an answer for all three questions. But for the rest of us, unless we've been intentional in our outreach, we may only be able to conjure up a face or two or three, but a name, let alone their marital status? No way. This, of course, is the point of this section. Paul wrote to the Colossians "Be wise in the way you act toward outsiders; make the most of every opportunity" (Col. 4:5). Let me say it again: shopping isn't just shopping—it's an opportunity. Whether you're shopping for jeans or jam and whether you're shopping at a locally owned, town-square store or at the mall, the Spirit is already going before you to break up hard hearts and souls. Your job is to be available and intentional.

Being Available

An old proverb says God isn't as interested in your ability as in your availability. Being available to do God's work is the first step to faithfulness, and it's the first step in sharing your faith. However, the problem with that old saw is that "being available" is often a cop-out for doing nothing. The local church has long claimed to be available to the local population simply by being a presence in the community. The act of "being a presence" too often means that the church building is open on Sunday mornings with a sign out front that reads, "Visitors Welcome." The church is available so long as guests are willing to walk through the doors between 10:45 and 11 o'clock (but don't be late lest everyone turn and notice the interloper). Being available means more than being approachable; it means to be useful, which implies being used. In other words, being available to God means being useful to God by allowing God to use you.

When it comes to sharing your faith, being available means more than just showing up—you need to be both aware and prepared.

Awareness comes back to the "quick" question: Who's the checker? A slew of invisible people populate our everyday world—people who serve us and without whom we'd be lost, but folks we simply don't notice. The greeter at Wal-Mart, the wait staff at Pizza Hut, and the checker at Walgreens. The key is to become aware of them—aware enough to care.

Being aware of those you meet isn't enough. It takes more than a courteous smile or a passing pleasantry to build a relationship with someone. Being prepared to begin a relationship means carving out a niche of time and space in your life for listening. Authentic listening is the foundation for any relationship. If you're going to be available, you need to be prepared for your schedule to be interrupted by the needs of others. Everyone has a story they desperately need to share with a sympathetic listener. It may be as simple as a "my car wouldn't start this morning" kind of story, or as complicated as "my spouse left me and took the kids last week." Whatever the story, by being available to those you've learned to see, you are demonstrating that you do care. Over time, if you will remain aware and prepared, your availability to make the most of every opportunity will arrive.

Being Intentional

I do the grocery shopping in our household most of the time. Although I shop in three different stores, I tend to do most of my shopping at Safeway just around the corner from us. The store is a rather large suburban grocery store that has well over fifty employees, but even so I've made it a point to get to know a number of them. Indeed, in some cases I have had the opportunity to share my faith because I've learned to make the most of the opportunities that have been presented.

The odds of any particular employee working when I shop is moderately remote, so building a relationship with any one of them has taken time. But that's what being intentional is all about—taking the time and making the effort to create opportunities for relationship building.

There are a number of ways you can build intentionality into your shopping, whether you're shopping for clothes, cars, or carrots:

1. Choose where you're going to shop carefully. Remember, where you shop can make an eternal difference. Shop where you have the greatest opportunity.

2. Be consistent about when you shop. I frequent Safeway on Monday afternoons because it's convenient to my schedule, but also because fewer shoppers tend to be in the store at that time. Additionally, some of the staff are on a regular schedule, so I can generally count on seeing Carl, Gary, and Candace there.

3. Consistently and intentionally choose your checkout. Whenever I'm done shopping and am ready to checkout, I look down the row of checkers and try to go through the line of someone I've been building a relationship with. For instance, if Gary's checking, I get into his line—even if it means I'll have to wait an extra couple of minutes. The first step to opportunity is familiarity.

4. Choose your conversation carefully. Most of us are conversationally programmed with meaningless small talk: "Hi. How are you today? Fine, thank you. It sure is hot today" and more banal chitchat. Making the most of our opportunities means making our conversations count. For instance, I don't know Candace well enough yet to begin conversation with personal questions, but I do know Leah that well. When Leah's my checker, I regularly ask about her brother and other members of her family. We may chat about church, and I've learned she doesn't go because she works late on Saturday nights and uses

Sundays to catch up on her sleep deficit. Our conversations continue to develop because I've been observant, modestly transparent, and intentionally interested.

These ideas work for virtually any kind of shopping you may be doing as long as you can develop frequency. Remember, familiarity breeds opportunity. Make an effort to get to know the checker, the waiter, the service station attendant, the produce manager, the pharmacist's assistant, the dry cleaner, the video store clerk, the front door greeter, the news vendor, the photo shop processor, and the bank teller.

Faith Sharing in the Marketplace

Okay, you've decided to make eternity-based choices about where to shop. You're committed to being available for the Spirit's leading in the marketplace, and you're willing to become intentional about how you're going to shop.

What now? How do you break the ice with the newsstand operator you've mostly been unaware of over the past five years? It's actually pretty easy. Because most vendors don't expect much more than basic civility from those they serve, if you make an extra effort you're not only going to get noticed, you'll be appreciated as well. Follow these three steps to move the level of conversation from civility to friendliness to spirituality.

Step One: Get out of the Crowd

Have you ever listened to the conversation at a busy checkout stand? Talk about conversational programming!

"Good morning. How are you?"

"That's good. Paper or plastic?"

"That'll be eighty-two forty. Debit?"

"Would you like cash back?"

"Twenty is your change. Thank you Mr. …..Brit-ee-an. You saved six thirty-seven today. Have a good day."

"Good morning, how are you?"

The only change in the conversation is when the checker recognizes the customer well enough to slightly personalize the banter (a rare occurrence) or when they actually know the customer and a real conversation takes place (even rarer). So anything you do that helps you stand out (in a positive way!) is a good start. The initial goal is to become a familiar face.

Here are some ideas for getting noticed—the first step to building a relationship.

Names. Dale Carnegie wrote that the sound of a person's name is the sweetest and most important sound in any language. Most of the "invisible" people who serve us wear name badges. Put face with name, and you've taken the first step. The ultimate test, though, is recognizing Carla the bank teller—and remembering her name—when she's outside the bank without a name tag on.

Courtesy. This should never have to be written in a book for Hitchhikers, but unfortunately it does. Service people have bad days. They make mistakes. They get sick. And they get blamed for circumstances beyond their control. Don't be one of the ones who complain—even under your breath. Smile. Be nice. Be patient. Be understanding. Be Wise! Make the most of every opportunity. When someone screws up, you have the choice to reflect grace or not. Don't *not*. Remember, the point is to become familiar in a positive way. (On the other hand, if their service is consistently horrid or you have a sense something else may be going on in their lives, talk quietly to the management, offering suggestions as helpful. Our job is not to get the person fired.)

Celebrate. Every day is a good day for a celebration—and our crazy national calendar offers more opportunities than you could ever hope to participate in. For instance, I'm writing this chapter in October. According to *Chase's Calendar of Events* this is National Pretzel Month, National Popcorn Poppin' Month, National Cookie Month, and the International Strategic Planning Month. Then there's Columbus' Day, National Boss's Day, and Halloween. Consider taking one of these celebrations and using it as an excuse for appreciation. Make a batch of homemade cookies and put three of them into a small plastic bag.

Then make a card that says "Happy National Cookie Month" (see illustration) with your name and contact information on the back of it, punch a hole in the card, and use a ribbon to tie it to the bag. The

next time you're shopping, after the standard checkout banter, give the clerk a bag of cookies, wish them happy cookie month, and be on your way. If the gift initiates a brief conversation, great. If not, don't worry about it. That will be one clerk who won't soon forget you! This sort of introduction can work year round. At Christmas I use full-size flavored candy canes with a card that has the story of the candy cane printed on it. I give them to drive-through attendants, bus drivers, bank tellers, store greeters, the checkers, and so on. These mini-celebrations open doors to conversations.

Step Two: Have a Conversation

Once you've made an impression and have become more than just another face in a sea of unending clients, it's time to begin a conversation. Remember two things about this step. First, if you've not made enough of an impression to be recognized as more than just another customer, go back to working step one. Second, it's more important to be interested than interesting.

Jennie Jerome was Winston Churchill's mother—an American citizen and a bit of a socialite. On one occasion she found herself seated for dinner next to William Gladstone, the leader of Britain's opposition party. The next evening she sat next to Benjamin Disraeli, Britain's Prime Minister. Asked her impression of the two men, she responded, "When I left the dining room after sitting next to Gladstone, I thought he was the cleverest man in England. But when I sat next to Disraeli, I left feeling that I was the cleverest woman in England." Gladstone was an interesting man, to be sure; but it was Disraeli's interest in Jennie Jerome that made all the difference for her.

Most people like to talk about themselves. Our culture bombards us with messages from all sides. Adults are exposed to over 3,000 marketing messages each day,[2] messages that are vying for our attention but give nothing in return. Additionally, the average American engages in about thirty conversations each day, with men speaking about 20,000 words and women about 30,000. That doesn't count the pseudo-conversations taking place in the grocery checkout line.[3] With all those words and messages rushing in on us, it's amazing anyone can get a word in edgewise. No wonder people are grateful to have someone actually listen to them. Just think, you have the opportunity to help make someone's day by being interested in someone besides yourself!

To begin a conversation with an acquaintance, you have to start off small; that is, start with small talk. Small talk is pretty much a lost art. We tend to practice it by indulging in insignificant chitchat to wile away the time—often in hopes that someone more interesting or more important will sidle by so we can engage in a real conversation. However, those adept at small talk know three secrets—everyone has an interesting story; no one is unimportant; and you are more charming when you're not talking than when you are—no matter what you might have to say.

The key to effective small talk is to develop three or four pertinent open-ended questions designed to help someone open up. An open-ended question is a query that can't be answered with a yes, no, or a grunt. A *pertinent* open-ended question is a query on a topic that might possibly matter to the person you're speaking to. For instance, chatting with your twenty-two-year-old hairstylist and asking whether they think Dewey's loss to Truman had a significant impact on the Second World War will probably lead to a dead-end response such as, "Huh?" (unless political history happened to be their major in college). On the other hand, you might get quite a flow of conversation if you ask, "I was reading a book this morning that said the average adult is exposed to over 3,000 marketing message every day. How do you think all that marketing is affecting us?" If you're standing in the checkout line at the grocery store, you might start a conversation by asking, "I just saw *Charlie and the Chocolate Factory* and really enjoyed it, even though I loved the original *Willie Wonka*. What's your favorite movie remake?" Now, granted, this second question isn't as open-ended as the first; however, the key to a successful conversation hinges on the quality of the follow-up questions. Asking, "In your opinion, what made [XYZ movie] better?" will hopefully kindle the conversation from spark to flame. To keep the conversation flowing, simply continue to ask open-ended follow-up questions that build on what's been said so far.

But good question asking is only about a tenth of the skill of small talk. Anyone can ask an open-ended question. Skillful conversationalists, however, are more than conversation starters. They're intent listeners. Remember Disraeli? Jennie Jerome did, but not because of his great accomplishments. Disraeli stood out in Jennie Jerome's mind less for what he said than because he listened intently. Perhaps because so many messages invade our consciousness, all too often we engage in conversation to be heard. Indeed, if we're not careful, we'll find ourselves in the midst of a conversation only half listening because we're busy formulating our responses. That's not listening, and it certainly isn't listening intently. Great conversationalists are those who practice listening, keeping their focus on the most important person in the world at that moment—the person who's speaking.

From Conversation to Friendship

Once you've begun conversing, the next step is to decide whether or not to invest in the relationship. We have a huge capacity for acquaintances. Although some suggest the average person has as few as 150 acquaintances, others assert that even introverts have at least 400 people they know. On the other hand, each of us has a limited capacity for close, significant friendships—friendships that allow us the opportunity to speak truth into one another's lives. Some may have the ability to have as few as five or six significant relationships at any given stage of their lives; others may have as many as nine or ten. Whether you can invest in four people or twelve, it's eternally important to choose prayerfully and carefully those whom you will offer your friendship.

By this time in the relationship you should know some basic information about the vendor you've been courting with conversation. Your small talk and careful listening should have provided you with their name as well as have given you a pretty good idea of their background. You will probably know where they grew up, some of their aspirations, hopes, and dreams, as well some of the their concerns. You should also have a sense of their spiritual state. Are they a Wanderer who has no real faith background or a Wanderer who has been misguided by another religious belief? Are they a Nomad who has been hurt by the church or a Nomad who has simply found the church irrelevant? Or are they a Hitchhiker who is faithfully practicing their beliefs? All this information will be helpful in making a decision about whether or not to invest further in a friendship.

But by this point you've gathered one more vital piece of information: whether or not you like this person enough to offer your friendship. If you do, and if this is a relationship where you can make an eternal difference, then take the next step to develop the friendship.

But What If...?

What if you already have five good friends, and you've established a fruitful conversational relationship with Ted the produce manager? Though Ted's a really nice guy who happens to be a Wanderer who's open to conversation about spirituality, the two of you just don't have enough in common to build a solid friendship. What if you're unable or if you intentionally choose not to take the relationship to the next level? Besides praying for them (and for God to send a worker into this particular harvest field—Luke 10:2b), what can you do? What *should* you do?

You can do several effective things. First, because you already have over 150 acquaintances, probably one of them is a Hitchhiker who could make a great connection with Ted. That acquaintance might be the answer to your Luke 10:2b prayer,[4] so make an intentional effort not only to introduce the two but also to facilitate a relationship between them. This can easily be done by providing a social context for the two of them to meet and get to know one another. For instance, host a backyard barbecue or a holiday get-together, invite them both to come, and make sure you introduce them in more than just passing.

If you're a part of a local church, a second thing you can do is invite Ted to a seeker event at your church. This might be a particular worship service, such as the kickoff to a relevant preaching series, or to an event such as an outreach party of some sort. Remember, Ted probably won't come along until you've invited him seven or more times. Whatever you do, though, don't invite him seven times to the same event—that would be both nagging and obnoxious; instead, invite him to a variety of church events over several months. When he does accept your invitation, make sure you're there to hang out with him and to introduce him to others.

Finally, if you're a part of a home fellowship group or another faith-based small group, invite Ted to join you. Again, you may want to wait for an opportune time to offer an invitation, such as when the group is hosting an open meeting or party, or when it is beginning a specific study series.

On-site Vendors

Some vendors you go to—the grocery store, gas station, pharmacy, dry cleaners, and so on. However, other vendors come to you (for instance, the vendor who steam cleans your carpet or cuts your grass). For those of you engaged in business or in the professional ministry, the on-site vendors in your life may include the copier tech, janitorial services, and a nearly endless supply of contractors. Like the marketplace vendors, you have the opportunity to make an eternal difference by the on-site vendors you choose.

The same questions for choosing a marketplace vendor come into play when you are selecting an on-site vendor, such as their faith status. However, consider other questions. For instance, will you have the opportunity to see the vendor often enough to build an ongoing relationship with them? Are they local enough so you can effectively invest in a friendship if you decide to?

Although you may be able to build a relationship with an on-site vendor in the same ways as you would a marketplace vendor, several differences warrant a few additional thoughts.

Discovering On-site Vendors

When I lived in a Midwestern rural community it was only a matter of months before I was well acquainted with virtually every vendor in town. However, urban and suburban dwellers will probably never get to know even a single-digit percentage of the vendors in their area. Finding a vendor with whom to make an eternal difference may seem like an impossible task.

O ye of little faith!

Two years ago, the church I was with decided to hire a Web site consultant to improve our Web presence. Hundreds, if not thousands, of vendors could have done this for us. Indeed, you can hire someone online to work on your Web site and never even lay eyes on the person. However, if you want to have an opportunity to make an eternal difference, proximity is almost always in order.

Begin your search with prayer. I'm not talking about a brief prayerful request as you're reaching for the Yellow Pages, but real, time-taking prayer. Ask the Divine to point you to the person that the Spirit has been preparing for your contact. Pray that you'll know where to turn and whom to contact, and that your search will be fruitful. You may even choose to pray *and* fast over the decision. Remember, this is serious business. Only after you've engaged this step are you ready for the next step.

Finding a vendor largely depends on referrals. Begin by asking your friends if they know someone who does what you're looking for. If they do, find out how well they know the vendor and whether or not they know their spiritual position. They may have no idea—discovering someone's faith stance isn't a typical topic of conversation, though perhaps it ought to be. The more prequalifying you can do before picking up the phone the more productive your search will be. If you don't have a referral from a friend, move on to your acquaintances. Malcolm Gladwell in *The Tipping Point* emphasizes that in these sorts of situations our acquaintances are often more helpful and influential than most other sources.[5]

However, the most fruitful referrals don't always come from friends or acquaintances. Sometimes we have to reach beyond our own circle of influence, to be missionaries of sorts, to be faithful. That's how I met Jeff, my Internet guru.

I began looking for Web site help by doing a Web search. In this case, I used Yahoo! Yellow Pages, a search engine that allows me to search for vendors located closest to my home address. The search referred me to several nearby vendors, but I noticed that one of them was actually located in my neighborhood. Of course, I knew nothing about this company, but a couple things I did know. First, when I visited the Web site I learned Jeff's name and saw his work. From what I could see, it looked like a quality product, so he made it past the first prequalifying step. Second, the Web site didn't have crosses, silver fish, or Bible quotes; so I was fairly sure the company wasn't specifically a "Christian" business (which didn't necessarily mean Jeff wasn't a Christian, but businesses that advertise their faith connection are nearly always operated by

Christians). Finally, because I live in a region where only 7 percent of the population is churched, I knew the odds were on my side that Jeff wasn't a churchgoing Christian. So I picked up the phone, called him, and made an appointment.

This wasn't just a Yahoo! referral, but a Divine appointment. Jeff wasn't a Christian. He and I were about the same age. We had some common interests. We were nearly neighbors. And, most importantly, we hit it off. Two years later, he and I are good friends. He's not a practicing Christian yet, but he's come from "I don't believe in God" to "Okay, I believe [assents to the 'facts']. I'm just really angry at the church." Sometimes it's a slow process, but Jeff might not even be in the process if I hadn't been choosy about my vendors.

Cultivating the Relationship

Once you've located a local vendor, the next step is to meet them, get acquainted, and make a decision about pursuing the relationship. Of course, one of the first issues you'll have to determine is whether or not you believe they can provide the services that you need. I'm not suggesting a charity call here—good stewardship of your resources demands that you hire someone who can do the job and do it correctly. You don't do anyone a favor by hiring someone who does substandard work.

Assuming the vendor can provide the service you need, spend some time during the get-acquainted interview to simply get a feel for the relationship's potential. This is an occasion to practice your small-talk skills—remember to ask open-ended questions, listen attentively, and follow up with more open-ended questions. This will give you feel for whether or not the two of you click.

For instance, Bob Coons is a church planter in Kentucky who was looking for a vendor to do some graphic design work for his church plant, The Journey. He found a local vendor, made an appointment, and once there, began the conversation. He takes up the story in his own words:

> I met yesterday with a person to do some graphic design stuff. I'm all business, trying to explain to him what I'm looking for him to do. At one point he said, "I'm not sure I want to do this…I'm not getting a handle on what you want…And I'm not much into church."
>
> He's our target age (mid to late 20s). He hasn't gone to church since he was seven. Mostly negative to apathetic feelings about church. Wasn't sure he wanted to do work for a church. You get the picture.

"Great," I said, "You're perfect! Here's what I want you to answer for me: What would a church have to look like or be like to have any attraction to you, or someone like you?"

Now, I've got his attention. "You're serious?" he asks.

"Yeah."

"Well, I guess it would basically have to not be a church."

I explained that's exactly what we're trying to do, plant a church that's not like a church (it has the essentials—a movement of people who follow Jesus, but doesn't have the church baggage).

Now, he's interested, too. We talk more. *Then* he says, "I'm still trying to get a handle on this. Would it be OK if I talk to my girlfriend and my buddies about it? None of them go to church, either." I'm guessing we'll be talking a lot more in the days to come.[6]

Bob was able to open a door for a meaningful conversation that may lead to an opportunity to take the relationship to the next level. Not only has Bob made inroads with this vendor, he's also made it possible to have a Hitchhiker's influence on the vendor's circles of influence.

When you are cultivating a relationship with a marketplace vendor, making contact with the acquaintance, and even the conversation level, is dependent primarily on their schedule. However, when working with an on-site vendor, contact is limited primarily by scheduling. In Jeff's case, I initially cultivated the relationship by scheduling a couple of meetings about the work he was doing. I always scheduled these get-togethers over either coffee or lunch (and I always paid). Of course, we'd talk about the Web site and the work that needed to be done, but I made sure business talk turned to real conversation. I asked questions about his job and how he ended up working on the Web. It turned out that we both had children attending the same school who knew each other, so we chatted about the school and eventually the family. Over the space of just three business meetings we had moved from a formal business relationship to friendly conversations. From there, we began getting together socially, and a friendship was born.

One of the issues when working with on-site vendors is how to advance a relationship from strict business to a social level. In Jeff's case it took very little effort on my part—but then, as I pointed out earlier, this was more a Divine affair with the Spirit's fingerprints all over it. More often than not, moving from business to social is a relatively slow process that regularly demands your intentional intervention. Much will depend on your prequalifying the relationship. If you don't hit it off, don't spend a lot of time pursuing the relationship beyond the business level. On the other hand, if you approach the relationship prayerfully, if your initial interview brings a level of openness and conversation, and if you have something in common besides the business at hand, the relationship may well blossom. Give it a chance by investing some time and effort.

A Word about Salespeople

Salespeople make a living selling. Although this may seem self-evident and even patronizing, we easily forget this fact when we're in the midst of interacting. Their job is to help make us comfortable and get us into a buying frame of mind. That being said, you may have difficulty discerning the difference between sales interest and genuine interest when you're trying to build a relationship. Someone in sales may be willing to meet us for lunch, coffee, and even visit our church in the hopes of making a sale—especially if the hopes are to make a rather large sale. In cases like these it can be far too easy to inadvertently abuse the relationship (on both sides).

People who know me can tell you that I'm not the most discerning guy in the world, and I had one of these experiences recently. I met Ted at an event for a nonprofit ministry that I supported. I was on the board and had a great relationship with the CEO who introduced us. Ted and I seemed to click, and we had a great conversation that evening. I gave him my card and told him about the house church I was involved in, and he expressed an interest. I didn't think much of it. I've discovered many people are curious about our church, and I didn't really expect to hear from Ted. However, the next week he gave me a call, and we met for coffee. We chatted, and I began to prequalify him to decide whether or not to pursue the next level of relationship. Ted was a Nomadic Christian. We talked about the church for quite awhile. In the conversation I also learned that he was in the insurance business, that he had a daughter in the military, and that he'd been divorced for several years. The relationship seemed to be moving along nicely, and I decided to cultivate the relationship.

Over the next few months Ted became active in our church. He and I would meet every couple of weeks for coffee or lunch. In time, however, it became clear that we were both abusing the relationship. Ted was primarily interested in selling me (and others at the church) insurance, but I was interested in becoming friends. But I didn't discern this difference early enough to put the brakes on gracefully. In the end, Ted went his way, and I went mine. I wasted a good bit of his time (I didn't have any intentions of buying more insurance), and I suppose in some ways my time may have been wasted as well (although time invested in a potential relationship, in my opinion, isn't wasted time).

The point is, when working with any vendor, but particularly with an on-site vendor, make sure that if you choose to pursue a social relationship, you have something to build on besides a sales pitch.

Every day you have choices to make that have eternal consequences: which grocery store you shop at and which checkout lane you choose; which restaurant you have lunch in and which server's section you sit in; which gas station you fill up at and whether you pay at the pump or interact with the cashier. The list is only limited by the number of choices you will get to make tomorrow. Practicing Hitchhikers of Jesus Christ don't have the option to take even these seemingly trivial decisions lightly. And though you can only invest in a limited number of significant relationships at a time, you're already balancing over 150 acquaintances. Some of these already have the Holy Spirit's fingerprints on them, and your name has been Divinely written in their spiritual appointment book. God's preparing them for your follow through.

Small talk, here we come!

By the Way Reflections

1. Quick, who greeted you the last time you went to Wal-Mart? Was the greeter male or female? Approximate age? Can you describe him or her? What was the greeter's name?
2. If you don't shop at Wal-Mart, what was the last store your visited? To which employees did you speak on your last trip there? Male or female? Approximate age? What did they look like? Names?
3. Whom do you know from your shopping excursions who is still unreached by Jesus? What are their names? If you don't know their names, write down three ways you might learn their names and use their names beyond the rote, "Thank you *fill-in-the-blank*."
4. Whom can you talk to about anything, knowing they will listen? Who relies on you to listen intently? What do you need to do to cultivate—or improve—these relationships?
5. Whom has God been preparing for you to cultivate a relationship with?
6. What relationships without friendship potential do you need to pass on to someone else? List three people you could introduce them to. How will you make those introductions?

NOTES

[1]See Appendix B for a list of forty New Testament one-another commands.

[2]Jack Fox, "Marketing in a Time-Scarce World," *SmartPros* (June 2002), http://accounting.smartpros.com/x34381.xml.

[3]Betty Lester, "A Little Instrument," TheChristianOnlineMagazine.Com, 2004. Do a search on the Web site for "Betty Lester" AND "instrument."

[4]The Luke 10:2b prayer is one of the few prayer requests Jesus tells us to pray: "The harvest is plentiful, but the workers are few. Ask the Lord of the harvest, therefore, to send out workers into his harvest field." This is a prayer God wants to answer in the affirmative!

[5]Malcolm Gladwell, *The Tipping Point* (New York: Little, Brown and Co., 2000), 54.

[6]Bob Coons, personal communication, November 10, 2005.

CHAPTER FOUR

Taking Jesus to Work

We are therefore Christ's ambassadors, as though God were making his appeal through us. We implore you on Christ's behalf: Be reconciled to God. (2 Cor. 5:20)

Once upon a time in what seems almost like another lifetime, I worked in a school. It was a one-room classroom with a wide range of students—from those I had to carry and change diapers for to seniors in high school studying advanced chemistry. The school itself was located in a metropolitan suburb and received oversight accreditation from the county school system—which meant that as a teacher I was bound under their rules. In other words, I was one of those state employees who wasn't allowed to bring faith into the classroom.

Hogwash! I didn't become a Christian so I could put the light under a milk bucket and sit on it. Faith isn't one of those things we get to take off and put on just because we walk onto our job site. I know a lot of people who try, but the fact is, our faith goes with us no matter what because faith determines the choices we make and the attitudes we take.

The average person in the United States or Canada will spend about 90,000 hours at work before finally punching out on the time clock of life. During that extended time, you and your faith are on display for all to see. You may be able to fool the church people an hour or two each week, but you can't fake out the folks who see you eight hours a day, five days a week, twenty-two days a month—they know you as you really are (scary, huh?). Your workplace is faith's litmus test. If your Christianity isn't on display there, well, let's just say you might want to take some time to evaluate what you say you believe.

Hitchhiking in the Workplace—Tethered to a Desk

Most people who work outside the home are tethered to their workplace. Whether they're in an office cubical, a classroom, on a factory line, or in a repair shop, they are committed to a particular space. If this is you, you have a number of unique opportunities to be an ambassador to your coworkers. However, before we get too far, let's take a peek at some of the more typical ways Christians respond in the workplace.

Stan is an auto technician, or better known as a mechanic. He's what I call a Closet Christian. He prays regularly, reads his Bible now and then, and both attends and is on the board of his church. However, according to Stan, he pretty much keeps his faith in the closet when it comes to work. I asked him why, and he shared with me a tale I'm all too familiar with. It went something like this:

> Back in the day of the silver fish on the back bumper, we used to dread whenever a "Christian" dropped off their car. We all tried to get out of working on their cars because we knew that if someone was going to complain or get ugly about the service or about the price, it would be the "Christian." Christians don't have a good reputation in the car business, so I keep my faith to myself. I know I can't be as good as I want to be, so I decided it's better to just keep quiet.

Frankly, I can sympathize with Stan. In some sense, it does seem better to not share your faith if you're unable to live up to it. Better to remain anonymous than to cast a shadow on Christianity. But three problems haunt this "solution."

First, none of us can live up to the ideals of Christianity. As we discussed earlier, the New Testament has over forty one-another commands that include being kind to one another, loving one another like Jesus loved us (a pretty tall order), encouraging one another, honoring one another, being devoted to one another, agreeing with one another, serving one another—you get the picture. Keeping these 100 percent of the time is out of reach. And these commands are how we're to treat other Christians who are supposed to be reciprocating. Loving our non-Christian friends and acquaintances "as ourselves" is even tougher yet, let alone loving our enemies. Keeping our Christianity closeted because we can't live up to the standards would mean Christianity never gets shared.

The second problem with Closet Christianity is that unless we're a name-only Christian, our coworkers already know we're a believer whether we want them to know or not. The fact is, over time we tend to drop clues about who we are in relation to our faith. We may inadvertently mention something about an event at church. We may make a comment about one of the Christian holidays. We might even "accidentally" quote something from the Bible. Remember that over the long haul, we're going to spend thousands of hours with some of our coworkers, which means they're going to get to know us well…very well. Whether we want it to or not, the Christian faith is meant to permeate our lives, and it has a way of seeping out.

That leads us to problem number three: Closet Christians send a mixed message. Although their coworkers may know they're Christians, their lives aren't much different than anyone else's—it's as if they're embarrassed to be believers. Unfortunately, many have *only* known Closet Christians, and so they've concluded that Christianity doesn't make much difference in people's lives.

On the other hand, there's Blaine. Blaine is what might be known as an over-zealous Christian. You can't be in the same room with him for more than ten minutes before you've deduced that he's a Christian. First, Blaine either wears a large cross around his neck so everyone can see it, or else he wears a branded T-shirt with bumper-sticker theology plastered all over it. His favorite outfit is a T-shirt proclaiming, in a well-known script, *Jesus is the Real Thing.* Second, Blaine punctuates every other paragraph with a hallelujah, praise God, or bless the Lord. Third, no matter what the topic of conversation may be, Blaine always finds some way to quote a Bible verse. Finally, Blaine is unapologetically in your face about *your* getting right with God: "*Now* is the time of God's favor, *now* is the day of salvation" (2 Cor. 6:2, NIV, emphasis added by Blaine). Blaine's style is, shall we say, overbearing.

Blaine and Stan are both Christians, yet their behaviors as Christians couldn't be more different; however, neither behavior faithfully represents Christianity. If Stan remains in the closet, the message he proclaims is that Jesus doesn't really make much of a difference. If Blaine remains over-zealous, the message he proclaims is that Jesus is, frankly, offensive rather than inviting. When practicing Hitchhiker's Evangelism, we must find some middle ground. Christians must be out of the closet but not in people's face. In other words, we have to find a "Hitchhiker who's traveling the Way" kind of evangelism.

Faithful Hitchhiking at Work

So, what's a Hitchhiker like at work?

Well, you may remember that a Hitchhiker, at least by our definition, is a practicing Christian. For the sake of this chapter, I'll add that a Hitchhiker is a follower of Jesus who is an unashamedly faithful believer, but isn't pushy with the faith.

Now, I realize *pushy* is a loaded word. What may seem pushy to one person may be innocuous to someone else. However, for the purposes of this chapter, let's say that a "pushy" Christian is like a stereotypical high-pressure used car (or vacuum cleaner, metal siding, vinyl windows, cell phones, and so on) salesperson. In other words, a pushy person responds to a "No thank you, I'm not interested" by switching closing tactics rather than by respecting the "No."

On the other hand, keeping the light hidden in the closet isn't the answer either. Hitchhikers share their faith, but they do so sensibly with a light touch. Paul wrote to the Colossians telling them, "Be wise in the way you act toward outsiders; make the most of every opportunity" (Col. 4:5). Let's use these instructions as an outline for the how-to of our faith sharing with "outsiders," that is, our coworkers and/or clients who are outside the faith.

The Foundation for Opportunities

Every worthy endeavor begins with a solid foundation of preparation, and that's no less true of Hitchhiker's Evangelism at work. The foundation of a building is stone or concrete; the foundation for a Hitchhiker is faithful living. Now, most of the time when I hear some preacher say something about faithful living, it's almost always in the context of doing "holy" things like attending worship, tithing, or serving on a church committee. However, faithful Way-faring is less about what you do *at* church and more about who you are and what you do in your "real life" (real life = the 167 hours or so per week you're not in a church building).

As I said earlier, you'll spend about 90,000 hours in the workforce during your lifetime. I call that the proximity factor. As a Hitchhiker that means your life is continually being examined, weighed, and measured by your coworkers, whether you like it or not, because of your proximity. How you treat clients, coworkers, subordinates, and superiors reflects not only on your personal faith, but on Christianity as a whole. Gandhi reportedly said, "I'd be a Christian if it weren't for the Christians I've met." These sentiments reflect a sad reality for many, especially for those in the workplace. Far too often, "Christians" press the boundaries of ethics and morality for the sake of the bottom line or to save face when they've made a mistake.

The early years of the twenty-first century saw a rash of corporate catastrophes brought on by dishonest, deceptive, and unethical business practices. The sad reality is that "Christians" sat at the helm of some of the biggest of these disasters (for example, Enron, HealthSouth, WorldCom). Too often, Christians at work have no better ethics and behave no differently than anyone else in the workplace.

In preparing for this section, I wrote a list of ten commandments for Hitchhikers at work. The more I looked at the list, the more uneasy I became, until something dawned on me: In the end, carefully keeping a list of rules doesn't make a Hitchhiker transparent, honest, and ethical. Rather, these are heart issues.

A story, perhaps apocryphal, about Alexander the Great applies here. On the eve of an important battle, the great general couldn't sleep. He decided to take a starlit stroll to think. As he wandered, he came upon a soldier who had fallen asleep at his post. Alexander quietly cleared his throat. The soldier was startled out of his sleep. Instantly recognizing the commander-in-chief, he felt a wave of terror crossing his face, for the penalty for his deed was execution.

Apparently, Alexander was in a charitable mood that night. Instead of calling for the soldier's arrest, he asked, "What's your name, soldier?" The soldier stammered out the words, "Alexander, sir." The general furrowed his brow, assuming the soldier had misunderstood the question. He asked again. "Soldier, I asked what is *your* name?" The soldier looked at the ground and replied, "Sir, my name is Alexander." At that, Alexander the Great stared intently at the miscreant soldier for some time, shades of disgust and anger rising and setting across his face. Then he turned on his heel and began to walk away, but not before saying, "Soldier, either change your ways or change your name."

Christians aren't perfect, but we've got to be more than just forgiven. When we carry the name of Christ, we are bound to a code of conduct: loving our neighbors, honoring our commitments, taking responsibility for our mistakes, and working for our employer as if we were working for the Lord. The foundation for Hitchhiker's Evangelism is faithful living. Without that, we can do little with the opportunities that may present themselves.

Opening the Gate for Opportunity

Paul expected Hitchhikers would find opportunities to share their faith on a consistent basis. The problem is, often we don't see the opportunities that come our way, or else they are few and far between.

We can alleviate both these issues by become more aware of opportunity when it knocks and by being more inviting so opportunity graces our door more often.

Pray for Opportunity

Prayer is often our last line of defense, but it is the only tool we have that safely connects us to the spiritual realm. Praying for opportunities to share our faith is one of the good-bet prayers—it's one you can be sure God wants to answer in the affirmative. Chapter 3 noted that God is less interested in our ability as in our availability. Praying for divinely initiated opportunities for faith sharing is a signal that we're available.

Create an Opportunity-Inviting Environment

Like the Opportunity Welcome Here illustration suggests, we need to be intentional in creating an inviting environment that attracts faith sharing opportunities. It all begins with subtle hints. Indeed, think *subliminal* when it comes to opportunity creation.

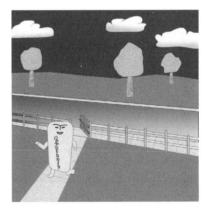

Begin with your physical environment. Whether you work in a cubical or out of a toolbox, if you have any control over some of your workspace, you can open the gates for opportunity to come knocking. For instance, when I'm writing at my local coffee shop, I tend to have a copy of my book *Prayer for People Who Can't Sit Still* sitting on the table. This has been one of the most effective "hints" I've found for saying—without saying—that I'm a Hitchhiker. The book is nonthreatening and has opened the door for many conversations (when I have my Bible out people tend to avoid eye contact, let alone approach me). Indeed, as I was writing this paragraph, a young man noticed *Prayer for People Who Can't Sit Still* next to me, came up, and excused himself for interrupting. We had an extensive conversation about the faith. As you can see, thoughtful decorating of even temporary space can open the gate for opportunities.

In a more traditional vein, Steve Necessary, the vice president of video product development for Cox Communications, has taken pains to lay out subtle clues to his faith by the way he's decorated his office. He has a Bible on his credenza and a painting of Jesus hangs on his wall across the desk from the business people who visit him there. It's nothing ostentatious, just a couple of simple reminders to himself about who he is. If others happen to notice and comment, "Why, that's an interesting painting," so much the better.

No matter what your career or where you work, you can decorate your environment to provide opportunities for faith sharing. Even in places with a clearly defined separation of church and state, such as in the school system or in state or federal offices, you are allowed a measure of personal expression that can open doors. Here's a list of ideas that people have used that may work in your setting.

- Place an icon in your space.
- Hang a reasonably sized faith-based painting or print in your space.
- Leave a faith-based book (this one!) on your desk where it can be seen.
- Put a faith-based desk or wall calendar in your office.
- Hang a set of prayer beads from the handle of your tool box, desk, or file cabinet.
- Keep a set of prayer beads on your desktop or workspace.
- Put a small labyrinth at your workstation.
- Burn a white unscented pillar candle while you're working.
- Quietly play a CD of Gregorian chant or your favorite Christian artist in your workspace.
- Set a small religious sculpture on your desk (I use a two inch high sculpture of the Lord's supper).
- Affix a magnetic crucifix, icon, or print to your toolbox.

You can find most of these items online or at your local Christian bookstore, while you can make others yourself if you're a craft-minded sort of person.

Don't despair if you don't have a specific workspace you can outfit with these hints; look for other ways to garner opportunities. Years ago, I worked as a cook in a twenty-four-hour restaurant. I didn't have a desk or any personal space that I could deck out with any faith-based hints. In cases like this, you can turn to personal adornment, that is, wearing symbols or emblems of the faith. Wearing branded products is common practice these days. Unless you're wearing a uniform that can't be embellished, you likely have some options for brandishing a faith hint.

Notice, however, the goal of personal adornment is to drop a hint, not to wear an in-your-face sandwich board. Generally, in-your-face faith statements are more confronting and offensive than curiosity invoking. Don't forget that the goal is to invite a conversation, not to provoke antagonism.

On the other hand, some Christian symbols have been so abused and overused that often they aren't recognized as uniquely Christian anymore and are unlikely to draw so much as a second glance. For instance, as many or more non-Christians are wearing jewelry with crosses on them as Christians are. WWJD bracelets and related products have been so common (as well as spoofed) that, although they may be great personal reminders, they hardly elicit notice. In other words, choose your faith accessories carefully.

Here's a list of some ideas for wearing your faith on your sleeve, so to speak:

- Wear a ring with a faith-based symbol on it.
- Wear a button with a faith-based symbol or saying on it—remember, the goal is subtlety.
- Put a faith-based zipper pull on your jacket.
- Wear faith-based jewelry such as a necklace or a bracelet—be creative, choose a crucifix over a cross, an anchor over a fish, and so on.
- Wear a shirt/blouse/jacket with a faith-based symbol embroidered on it—again, subtle and uncommon enough to raise a question.
- Put a Christian fob on your keychain.
- Put a Christian charm on your charm bracelet.
- Wear a brooch with a meaningful symbol on it.
- Wear a wristwatch with a Christian design (some have designs on the faces, others on the wristband).
- Wear a hat with a faith-based symbol or saying on it.
- If you do tattoos, consider wearing one with a meaningful symbol (see chapter 7, "Getting Radical" for more on this).

Whether you adorn your office space with a couple of faith hints or wear an embroidered Celtic high cross on your sleeve, the goal is to get a coworker, client, or even a passerby to ask about it. Whenever they do, an opportunity has graced your presence for better or for worse, which is what the next section is all about.

Making the Most of Every Opportunity

"Knock, Knock."

"Who's there?"

"Opportunity."

"'Tis not—Opportunity doesn't knock twice."

Or so the old joke goes. The apostle Paul's reminder to make the most of every opportunity we get with "outsiders" is a critical reminder—we may not get two chances. Far too often, we're so caught up in our own personal world that opportunities to share our faith blur by without our notice. Indeed, that's one of the most important reasons why prayer is the first and most important gate-opening tool. Prayer doesn't just let God know of our availability, it also heightens our sensitivity to even the faintest raps at the door.

Even lifelong churchgoers too often don't recognize opportunities to share their faith when they appear. And when they do recognize them, they may not know how to respond effectively. Let's look at a four-step process that may be helpful.

1. Recognize Opportunity

Opportunity tends to show up in one of three ways. Sometimes you'll be presented with an opportunity that can hardly be missed, the old two-by-four–up-the-side-of-the-head kind of opportunity. Someone may sidle up to your workstation and say, "I've been noticing that you're the kind of person people can talk to. I've been really struggling with my faith. Can we talk?" I think the only way anyone misses an opportunity like that is to intentionally ignore it.

The second kind of opportunity is interest opportunities. Hearing these timid knocks is not quite as easy as recognizing the two-by-four opportunities; however, if you've been praying for and anticipating them, they're fairly obvious. For example, if you've hung a set of prayer beads on your toolbox and the mechanic who works in the next bay asks, "So, what's with the beads?" you've just been given an opportunity to share your faith. The same goes with someone who asks about the Celtic goose embroidered on your shirt (an ancient symbol of the Holy Spirit). Anyone who expresses interest in one of your spiritual hints has offered you an opportunity to share.

I call the third kind of opportunity issue opportunities. These can be the most difficult to identify and the easiest to miss. Everyone has issues. Whether someone is just having a bad day or their life is falling apart, when someone shares a life issue with you, they've taken a stroll down opportunity lane—but you have to be alert to hear the opportunity in the conversation.

In 1967 Thomas Holmes and Richard Rahe published an article that rated the level of trauma in people's lives.[1] Life's traumatic events were given a rating from 1 to 100 based on how much stress they caused. For instance, the most traumatic event according to Holmes and Rahe is the death of a spouse followed by divorce, marital separation, jail time, and so on.

This rating has been widely used to "measure" the readiness of someone to hear and receive the Gospel. When we experience a traumatic issue in our lives, we have a tendency to start looking for the meaning behind it. We ask the why question and look for answers. Sometimes we want solutions to our problems, but often what we really want and need is a word of hope. When a coworker opens

Life's Traumatic Events	Stress Score
Death of a spouse	100
Divorce	73
Marital separation	65
Jail Term	63
Death of a close family member	63
Personal injury or illness	53
Marriage	50
Fired at work	47
Marital reconciliation	45
Retirement	45
Change of family member's health	44
Pregnancy	40
Gain of a new family member	39
Change in financial state	38
Death of a close friend	37
Change to a different line of work	36
Change in number of arguments with spouse	31
Foreclosure	30
Change in role at work	29
Child leaves home	29
Begin or end school	26
Change in living conditions	25
Change in residence	20
Christmas	12

up and says, "I just found out my husband lost his job" or "Would you keep my mom in prayer, we just found out she has cancer?" you've been given an opening to share your faith.

2. Acknowledge Opportunity

When you recognize the knock of opportunity, the first thing to do is to acknowledge it—which is to say, you open the door. However, before you put your hand on the doorknob, take a brief moment to offer a silent prayer for support. All too often, we meet opportunity in our own strength and in our own way. When we do, we run the risk of blowing it completely. Whenever an opportunity presents itself, take a couple of nanoseconds to ask the Spirit to take over.

3. Welcome Opportunity

I don't know if my grandma said it or not (but if she didn't, she should have): "God gave you two ears and one mouth to use in that proportion." The key to wisdom has always been listening, and that's never more true than when it comes to making the most of every opportunity. People need to be heard and want to be understood. Far too often, we're misquoted and maligned because we weren't understood in the first place. So before you launch into solving an issue, illuminating an interest, or waxing eloquent when the two-by-four opportunity hits you, take the time to make sure you understand the issue or the question at hand.

4. Respond

Here's where the wheels of wisdom meet the road of reality. Opportunity has rung your doorbell! You've heard it, looked through the peephole, whispered a prayer, opened the door, and stretched your arms to welcome it with understanding. Now it's time to open your mouth and share the reason for the hope you have with your friend, relative, acquaintance, neighbor, or coworker. Exactly what you say depends on many, many things, not the least of which is the Spirit's leading. However, the goal of your conversation is to either plant a few seeds, to further cultivate a sprouting faith, or to reap a harvest, depending on where the person is on the spiritual journey.

Although chapter 8 deals with the specifics of sharing your story, I want to introduce here some of the guidelines for responding wisely to opportunities.

The first guideline is to be bold without being obnoxious. Paul reminded Timothy that we were not given a spirit of timidity; instead, we are given the exact opposite of that. Paul doesn't define this boldness in terms of brashness or being overbearing. Instead, he defines boldness as the spirit of power, love, and self-discipline. When you step up to an opportunity to share your faith, know that you are stepping up in the divine power—but that power is borne of love and self-discipline. That love remembers that this opportune encounter is not about me, but about the one who is seeking. This self-discipline remembers you have two ears and one mouth, to be used in that proportion.

The second guideline is to be subjective rather than objective. This probably sounds counterintuitive for those who've been raised in a church where various scripture passages have been used either to prove a point or to support an assertion. Now, there's nothing wrong with doing this in a setting where everyone agrees that the Bible is an authoritative source; however, those who aren't a part of that faith tradition tend to look at the Bible as "just another religious book." Pointing to a verse and saying, "This verse proves that Jesus is the son of God" doesn't prove anything to someone who thinks the Bible is on par with *Chicken Soup for the Soul.* Indeed, objective answers are more likely to lead to a disagreement or an argument. If you get into an argument, you will lose even if you "win." On the other hand, no one can argue effectively against your personal experiences. Your relationship with Jesus is your testimony, your witness. The early apostles who took the Way to the Gentiles didn't have any scriptures they could use—the New Testament didn't exist, and non-Jews did not recognize the Old Testament as having any kind of authority. If they could effectively introduce the faith without citing chapter and verse (and they did), so can you!

The last guideline is arguably the most important: remember that you don't have all the answers. No one expects that you do. I can't tell you why my daughter, who wanted to have a large family, had to have a hysterectomy after the birth of her first child and can't have any more children. Nor can I tell you why I have ADHD, but God called me to sit still long enough to write books anyway. I can't even do a very good job trying to explain the Trinity. I don't have all the answers, and neither do you. I'll confess that I hate this about myself. I like being the answer guy. But I've learned that the most effective way to share my faith is to be humble when a question is beyond me.

Wanderers and Nomads (and many Hitchhikers, for that matter) are tired of hearing from people who think they speak for God and don't, and from people who think they have it all figured out, which they don't. In the words of a great postcard, "People who have all the answers don't allow questions." You will sway more hearts with an air of humility, with an admission you don't have an answer, than you will by blustering your way through.

The notion that every question has an answer is a fallacy anyway. We're not God, so many things we just don't know, can't find out, and wouldn't understand if we could. When a coworker asks you, "Why would a good God allow bad things to happen to good people?" you're generally better off quietly saying, "I don't know, I really don't. But I do know God's always been there for me even in the worst of times" instead of explaining that the only "good" person who ever lived was crucified, or that the only alternative to allowing evil is to suspend free will. If they seem to want to continue the discussion, you can turn to the New Testament and look at some of those who suffered and what they had to say about it (Rom. 5:3–4; Jas. 1:2–4; Acts 14:19–22; 2 Cor. 11:23–30).

Making the most of every opportunity with your coworkers ultimately means building a meaningful and lasting relationship with them, a relationship that opens the doors to conversations about your faith and, ultimately, about Jesus Christ.

Hitchhiking in the Virtual Office

According to some accounts, less than 25 percent of the North American workforce enjoys the relative "freedom" of virtual officing. Some of these workers are in sales, while others work for companies that have discovered the benefits of mobile, decentralized employees. Others are self-employed and work when and where they please, at least to some extent. If you're one of the "lucky" ones, the rest of this chapter is for you.

Office Where the Heart-Burst Is

Matthew 9 tells of Jesus going from town to town, village to village to teach and to heal. As he looked over the crowds, "He had compassion on them, because they were harassed and helpless, like sheep without a shepherd" (Mt. 9:36). These people made Jesus' heart ache—they were his heart-burst. Heart-bursts are those people your heart is moved for, whether they be the down-and-outs, the terminally ill, a particular generation, a profession, or the folks in your neighborhood. My heart bursts for those who have been turned off or hurt by the church. I spend many of my waking hours either in prayer about them, spending time with them, or training others (like you!) how to share the Gospel with them.

So who's your heart-burst?

In my little world I've discovered that some of the people I most desire to reach often hang out at a Starbucks near my home. Because my schedule is fairly flexible, I'm able to take my laptop there and "set up shop." I've written the bulk of three books at that coffee shop, and I've had the opportunity to share my faith almost weekly with someone there. Sometimes, a complete stranger approaches me, and I get to share. At other times I have an opportunity to share with someone I've built a strong relationship with. The point is, I get opportunities to share my faith because I office in the midst of my heart-burst.

Where do you office?

While I'm at Starbucks, I have the opportunity to see quite a number of men and women who enjoy the freedom of virtual officing. Some are in sales, some in information technology, while others are teachers who stop in regularly to grade papers, develop lesson plans, and so on. The local coffee shop isn't the only place where you can work and meet your heart-bursts at the same time. You have to answer who your heart-burst is before you can decide the most effective place to work and to practice Hitchhiker's Evangelism.

For instance, if you're personally interested in sharing your faith with the homeless in your community, you may want to set up office at the local library. In most metropolitan areas, many of the homeless find their way to the library to peruse the newspaper or the Internet for jobs, as well as to find a safe place to hang out. If you office in the library, you can both work and make yourself available to your heart-bursts. On the other hand, if your heart bursts for college students, you'll want to consider officing on a college campus. If your heart bursts for dock workers, you can office at a coffee shop, bar, or café near the wharf. Where you office is limited only by your creativity. My wife has pursued studies in an alternative method of healing as a way to engage those who are exploring New Age and non-Christian faith practices. The key is to identify who your heart bursts for, discover where they hang out, and then get intentional about virtual officing in that locale. The goal is to be visible and to be available.

Hitchhiker's Evangelism at your virtual office is nearly identical to Way-faring in a fixed work environment, except that you're limited in the amount of decorating you can do! Still, when I'm at Starbucks, I do what I can. As I said earlier, I keep an interesting spiritual book on the table while I work. Recently, I loaned my daughter a copy of Anne Rice's *Christ the Lord: Out of Egypt* to read while commuting on the bus. She commented that she's had more people interrupt her reading to ask about the book than with anything else she's ever read. People in a friend's Twelve Step group regularly comment on the colorful book bag she purchased at a church gathering. These interruptions might better be labeled opportunities just begging for a conversation about faith.

A Special Word to Pastors

I've served a number of churches over the past twenty years or so and know the pressure from some well-meaning congregants who want you to keep extensive office hours in the church office. Pastors do need to spend some time in the pastor's office, but we tend to spend way too much time behind closed doors as if we were monks or nuns in a cloister. Nearly every pastor I know confesses a sense of frustration about their ministry. They got into ministry to introduce people to Jesus and to equip others to introduce people to Jesus, but when they work in a church office the only people they see are churched people. Unfortunately, the unchurched, by definition, don't hang out at church.

Getting out of the office and into the harvest field can be a gutsy move for most pastors. Someone in the congregation always seems to expect the pastor to be in the office and ready to greet them should they ever decide to drop by the church building. Often these people have a lot of power or control in the church. Rather than bucking the system, we tend to cave in. We pray in our office. We research and write our sermons in the office. We hold meetings in our office. We write newsletter articles in our office. We make phone calls in our office. We spend a *lot* of time in our office. And while we may make a few parishioners happy by being available there, the sad fact remains: we won't reach any Wanderers or Nomads from our office spaces. To practice Hitchhiker's Evangelism we've got to escape and spend time in the real world.

Virtually none of the activities we accomplish in our offices necessitate an office environment. We can pray nearly anywhere. Sermons can be researched and prepared at the library. Many, if not most, meetings can be held at a local restaurant. The newsletter can be written at a coffee shop. We don't have to be sequestered in an office to be productive. When we get out of the office, we're more available and accessible to the unchurched in the community.

Over the past three years, I've spent 90 percent of my office hours in public places. We've even held board meetings at Starbucks. I simply forward the church phone to my cell, pack up my laptop, and away I go. Except for counseling appointments, I meet with my congregants either at their workplaces or at a nearby coffee shop or café. The churched know where to find me and, not surprisingly, so do the unchurched friends and acquaintances I've made over the years.

So, pastor, draw a line through office time and scrawl the name of your local book store, coffee shop, bar, library, or restaurant on the schedule. Then head out into the fields—as Jesus said, they're white unto harvest.

By the Way Reflections

1. Would you categorize yourself as a "Closet Christian" or as a Hitchhiker?

2. The American church has an abundance of Closet Christians. Why do you think there are so many? What could you or your church do to embolden the ones in your church?

3. Every day, Hitchhikers are faced with moral and ethical dilemmas at work. Describe a time when you struggled ethically or morally over a decision you had to make. What can your church do to equip people like yourself to better apply their faith to their decision making?

4. What are some ways you can facilitate faith-sharing opportunities in your workplace? On your person?

5. What is the biggest struggle you have with sharing your faith? How could your church better equip workers like yourself in effective faith sharing?

6. Who is your heart-burst? What can you do to spend significant time with them? What can you do to facilitate faith-sharing opportunities with them?

NOTES

[1]Thomas Holmes and Richard Rahe, "Social Readjustment Rating Scale," *Journal of Psychosomatic Research* 11, no. 2 (1967): 213–18.

CHAPTER FIVE

ENOF Is Enough

Ending Segregation

The kingdom of heaven is like yeast that a woman took and mixed into a large amount of flour until it worked all through the dough. (Mt. 13:33)

"Eleven o'clock is the most segregated hour in America," said Billy Graham in the 1950s. What was true then remains true today. During the Civil Rights Movement, Martin Luther King Jr. quoted Graham regularly as he fought for equal rights. Over fifty years later, the mainline denominations continue a hue and cry about racism in the so-called melting pot. According to many church leaders, the segregation of race is the evil dragon that most needs to be slain in the church today.

It's not. Contrary to popular opinion, race is not the most pervasive venue of segregation in the North American church. According to a Gallup poll, more than 243 million people claim to be Christian in the United States. Of these, approximately 14 percent are Hispanic, 12 percent are African American or Black, 1 percent are Asian, and less than 1 percent are members of other minority races. That leaves about 72 percent who are Anglo or White. The reality is, U. S. Christianity is more diverse than our nation, which is 75.6 percent White.[1] However, Billy Graham is correct that few congregations reflect significant racial diversity—most congregations reflect a fairly homogenous ethnicity. And yet, most individual congregations try to be welcoming to other races and ethnicities when the opportunity arises. Racial segregation is a fact, but not generally by design.

On the other hand, a fierce dragon threatens the North American church. This dragon is more dangerous than the dragon of racial segregation. This particular dragon has imprisoned the church in an impregnable tower that few dare to assail. Once we find ourselves in the tower, few manage to escape.

Who, pray tell, is this vicious dragon? The most evil dragon of segregation is the one that segregates the One-Anothers from the Everyone-Elses. The more critical problem lies, however, not in the fact that they are segregated from each other on Sundays at eleven: The other 167 segregated hours during the week are the problem.

Oh sure, we work in the same office building, shop at the same stores, eat at the same restaurants, ride the same buses, and even drink from the same drinking fountains. For all the world, it looks like believers intermingle with non-Christians (except on Sundays at eleven), but this dragon of Christian segregation is much more insidious.

Church growth scholars have long established that in the United States and Canada the average new Christian convert is only evangelistically effective for about six months. After that, the effectiveness typically drops to nil. Why? What happens at the six-month mark that is crippling the church?

The answer is the dragon of Christian segregation. Let's use Donna as an example. Donna's life was in turmoil when a thoughtful friend invited her to visit a Saturday evening home fellowship group. During the meeting she heard story after story of what God was doing in these people's lives. In a tearful torrent, she broke down, confessed that her life was out of control and that she wanted nothing more than to be in God's grace and under God's care. Her friend and the home fellowship group gathered around her and prayed with Donna. When they finished, Donna experienced the peace of God's presence with an overwhelming flood of relief. Her enthusiasm and excitement over her newfound faith could hardly be contained.

Whenever a new believer makes a commitment to being a faithful Hitchhiker, the dragon of Christian segregation begins to inflict itself on the new believer's life. First, on Sunday morning, the larger church warmly and firmly embraced Donna. They invited her to sing in the choir. Her new friends took her to their Sunday school class where she enrolled. She was, of course, invited to become a permanent part of the Saturday night home fellowship group. Then the women's fellowship president invited her to a mission's Bible study on Tuesday evenings. Members also encouraged Donna to become active in the food drive the church was having to fill the Thanksgiving baskets they would be putting together in the fall. Oh yes, she was also invited to the new member's introduction dinner, for coffee with the pastor, and to the church's upcoming potluck and dinner theater (wouldn't she like to audition for a part in the next play?). Now, all this seems good and right, if not slightly overwhelming. Most of these invitations seldom come altogether on a single Sunday, but inevitably, these sorts of invitations for involvement do get made. As you can see, Donna is going to be busy, though she will be well cared for and her faith will be nurtured by her newfound Christian family.

But let's continue Donna's story. At work on Monday morning, Donna, filled with excitement over her newfound faith, began to share with her friends. Some listened politely, others scoffed and rolled their eyes, and a few asked genuine questions about what she experienced. Two even came with her to church, and one became an active member. However, by the end of a couple months, Donna had shared her experience with virtually everyone she knew. Her friends, relatives, acquaintances, neighbors, and coworkers had all heard her story. Donna's opportunities for sharing her faith diminished.

Donna's story illustrates well how the dragon of Christian segregation accomplishes its scheme. First, the dragon rallied the church to enfold its arms around Donna so warmly and lovingly that she gave herself willingly into its care. She made new friends, all of whom were fellow believers, so she had little time for socializing with her old friends in the unchurched culture from which she came. Though Donna had been a volunteer at a community food bank, she discovered that her church sponsored a Christian food bank and so she got involved there instead.

Donna's immersion into her faith and her church effectively removed Donna from the unchurched world. She no longer had time for her unchurched friends; besides, she didn't have much in common with them anymore. She was also effectively insulated from the rest of the unchurched world: She no longer spent time with the Wanderers and Nomads at the community food bank, nor at the clubs she used to frequent, nor at any of the places she used to spend her free time. By the end of six months, Donna's conversion was complete—she was completely "churched" and completely segregated from the unchurched. The dragon of Christian segregation had struck once again.

When Jesus commissioned his followers to make disciples, he didn't say, "Go ye therefore to construct church buildings, post informative and attractive signage, and engage in effective marketing campaigns to entice people to visit." On the other hand, he did say "go and make disciples" (Mt. 28:19), which can be literally translated, "As you're going," that is, "While you're hitchhiking through life." Look carefully, and you'll see an implied assumption in the Great Commission: Hitchhikers will be out there in the world, rubbing shoulders with the Everyone-Elses.

The rest of this chapter is divided into two sections. First, we'll make an honest assessment about where we are when it comes to interacting with the world outside our church walls. Only when we figure out where we are can find our way back. Second, we'll address one of the most prevalent questions asked by well-churched Hitchhikers: What do I do if I don't know any unchurched?

When Is Enough Church Enough?

Donna's story is typical for the way the church has worked for a long time. Although most people who become new Christians don't experience quite the rush of activities Donna did, most new Christians who get involved in a church end up isolated from the real world in less than six months. If we don't have any unchurched friends, how can we be faithful to the Great Commission?

That coin has another side. Hitchhikers really need to be involved, even highly involved, with the church. Christianity is a team sport—without any place for solo practitioners. Paul used the metaphor of the body in 1 Corinthians. Even with all of today's advances in medical science, no single part of the body can survive by itself. The heart needs the lungs, the brain needs the spinal cord, the ear needs the nose, and so on. Not one part of the body can function on its own. Even a cursory glance at the early church in the book of Acts can make Donna's experience of being over-churched look almost normal. According to Acts 2:42–47 the first church members (1) devoted themselves to the apostles' teaching; (2) devoted themselves to the fellowship; (3) met at the temple courts daily; and (4) ate their meals together nearly everyday as well. With all that, you would think they had neither the time nor the energy for nonbelievers. But verse 47 dispels that notion: "And the Lord added to their number daily those who were being saved." Clearly the new believers were spending time with their unbelieving friends, relatives, acquaintances, neighbors, and coworkers.

Which begs the following questions: When is enough church enough? How do we juggle our involvement in the church world with the "real" world?

When Too Many Feathers Flock Together

From the beginning of the church, believers hung out together. In a world hostile to the claims of Christianity to the point of hunting down these wayward heretics and imprisoning or even executing them, it was comforting, if not outright safer, to enjoy the company of other like-minded people. Birds of a feather flock together, but oftentimes they suffer from excessive flocking.

Have you ever noticed that only rarely will you see multiple breeds of birds sharing the same wire? That's not coincidental—that's nature.

Let's face it, overall people like being with those who believe like us, act like us, and even look like us. Indeed, being with others who have significant differences generally makes us pretty uncomfortable, that is until we find enough common ground to ease our disease. Donald McGavran, the father of the church growth movement, called this the homogeneity principle. Like attracts like in almost every aspect of creation except magnets and marriage. It's not just human nature, it's nature…period.

Good things happen when believers spend significant time together, and I don't in any way want to suggest otherwise. Proverbs remind us that as iron sharpens iron, one person sharpens another (Prov. 27:17). Hitchhikers must spend time with each other for accountability, discipling, training, and encouragement. But when we spend all our time in our own flock, we run the risk of becoming inbred, isolated, and so heavenly minded that we're no earthly good. Indeed, one of the chief reasons the passenger pigeon became extinct was because of its penchant for excessive flocking.

Passenger pigeons loved their own company. Their flocks were huge; millions of birds lived together, ate together, and migrated together. (In 1866, a flock of passenger pigeons a mile wide and 300 miles long flew over Ontario—it took fourteen hours to pass a single point. Estimates suggest there were nearly 3.5 billion birds in that single flock.[2]) However, because they were so group oriented, they were easy targets for hunters. A single shotgun could easily bring down twenty or more birds. For a time, the culinary demand for the bird was so high that it became quite lucrative to hunt the birds. It wasn't a difficult task, because they flocked so tightly together. Some hunters would keep a "pet pigeon" to use as bait to attract a flock into shooting range. They would tie the bird to a post or a stool in the middle of an open field. When a passing flock heard the "stool pigeon's" cry and saw its awkward flapping, the flock would change course to investigate and to congregate around the lone bird. As they did, of course, they were harvested by the thousands.

The point is that excess flocking isn't always beneficial, and it can be deadly.

When We Become Phobiacs

Many folks mistakenly believe they suffer from acrophobia, the fear of heights. They think because they don't want to crawl over to the edge of the Grand Canyon and look straight down, they suffer from a phobia. But that's not a phobia; that's plain common sense. If you get too close to the rim, you might fall over. Or if you climb up on your peaked roof, you might slip. Or if you climb to the top of a tall ladder, you might lose your balance. There's something about having a healthy respect for potential danger.

A phobia is something else again. A phobia is an irrational fear that persists even when we're aware we're safe. Phobias often lead to panic or intense and abnormal self-protection. Sometimes I think the church suffers from *apistoi-phobia,* the irrational fear of unbelievers.

Funny how God works. As I began this section, I got a phone call from one of my daughters who, after a long absence, just recently became active in a local church. Apparently she had gone out to a pub on New Year's Eve with some of her unbelieving friends. Although she acts with integrity wherever she is and whomever she is with, some members of her church small group severely chastised her for spending time in such an unchristian environment with unchristian friends. And why were these well-meaning Christians so concerned about my daughter's friends and whereabouts? Because they were afraid her unchurched friends might influence her negatively. Sadly, no one even considered that she might influence them positively.

Let me assure you that I'm not advocating that every Christian should rush down and start hanging out in the clubs and bars. Some Hitchhikers are recovering alcoholics or addicts and could find the temptations too enticing. On the other hand, for many who express indignation over the suggestion that a Hitchhiker might be okay in a bar, the issue is generally *apistoi-phobia.* But in the words of a friend of mine, "If the church is going to reach the lost, we're going to have to start sitting in the smoking section."

We should have a healthy concern about hanging out in dens of temptation. A plethora of temptations lurk in every bar, club, and unchurched neighbor's house. Everywhere we go outside the church walls can tempt us with intemperance, gluttony, lust, adultery, and so on. On the other hand, a plethora of temptations lurk behind every church gathering as well: gossip, pride, vanity, and gluttony—even lust and adultery are temptations within the body of Christ. We literally have no place on earth to go to escape temptation—even the monastics do regular battle with it.

Jesus taught that disciples are supposed to be salt, yeast, and light. But salt's not much good unless you get it out of the saltshaker. Yeast is pointless in an hermetically sealed package. A flashlight doesn't do much good in the sunshine. All of these metaphors imply that Christians are meant to make a difference in the world, not by setting up protective forts that insulate us from the Wanderers or the Nomads, but by stepping into their space and being an influence there. Good shepherds don't stand at the pen's gate and call out "Where are you, O lost sheepy, sheepy, sheep? You can come home now." As Jesus pointed out, the good shepherd leaves the ninety-nine and goes searching in the big, bad, threatening world to rescue the wandering lambs.

Should we be frightened? No. Should we be wary? Yes. But then, that's the difference between an unhealthy phobia and a healthy respect.

Get Grounded without Being Grounded

The answer to excessive flocking and the fear of being unduly influenced by the "world" is to be well grounded without being grounded.

I remember all too well getting grounded by my mom and dad when I was guilty of some misdeed or another (like not cleaning my room). In our house, being grounded meant we were restricted to the house and sometimes even to our rooms. Being grounded was akin to the restrictions of being under house arrest, except we didn't get to use the phone, watch television, or anything else that would wile away the time. The point of being grounded was to teach us a lesson and keep us out of further trouble. Being grounded wasn't fun.

I suppose that if we had been well-grounded, obedient children all the time we would never have been grounded. Our parents would have had no need to ground us. The same holds true in Way-faring. If we are well grounded in the faith, we have no need to be grounded to the church, which, of course, creates a tension. How do we, as the light of the world, get grounded well enough to withstand temptation when we leave the safety, security, and watchfulness of our fellow Christians?

Let's begin with Myth Busting 101. A long-standing myth claims that Christians should sequester themselves with the company of other Christians to escape temptation. A second myth, equally long-lived, is that before a believer can "survive" the temptations of the world, he or she must first become a deeply-rooted, mature, faith- and spirit-filled practicing Christian. If that were true, Christianity would have died of loneliness 2,000 years ago because none of the believers would have ever left home. As I said before, no one ever gets beyond temptation—no matter how mature you are and no matter how remote the monastery you try to hole up in. Although the kind of temptations we face may vary between the bar and the Sunday school classroom, temptations never go away.

The answer to faithfulness in the world is to be grounded. Let me explain what I mean by *being grounded*. You may have heard the phrase "being grounded in the Word" or something like that. That kind of grounding means having a great deal of knowledge and understanding of the scriptures, and thus being well grounded in the faith. The problem is that being well versed in the Bible does not make a mature, well-grounded Hitchhiker. At least, not if the examples in the New Testament have anything to say about it. Paul started the Thessalonian church in just three weeks—and left it in the hands of the new converts (Acts 17). Today in India, China, Indochina, and Africa, brand new Christians are setting out to other towns to start new churches through evangelism, and many of these effective new evangelistic Hitchhikers are illiterate. They don't even own a Bible, let alone know how to read one. Being grounded in the faith is not about knowledge.

The kind of grounding I'm talking about is like a car battery that's grounded to the car's frame. As long as the battery is connected to the frame, the car will start, the lights will light, and you can drive away. But if the battery's grounding cable is weak or if it becomes disconnected, then even the car's clock can't tick. For Hitchhikers, being grounded means having a solid connection with the body of Christ. That connection is more than just going to church. It's more than just singing in the choir or playing in the band. It's even more than segregating yourself from the world and hanging out nearly exclusively with a clique of Christian friends. Being grounded means being in a deeply committed, accountable spiritual friendship. I call that kind of spiritual friend an accountability partner.

Now, an accountability partner is someone who is more than just another friend who happens to be Christian. An accountability partner is a fellow Hitchhiker; a close, personal friend; a confidant; a confessor; a spiritual mentor; someone you trust completely; and someone who has permission to speak truth into your life. Someone who knows you well enough to see through you when truthfulness wanes.

If you're going to be out in the world, you need this kind of a friend who will meet with you weekly to help you stay on the Way. Because the point of this weekly get-together is accountability, having some sort of an agenda is helpful. I'd suggest using the Journey Group Partnership that's outlined in the next chapter. By being open and honest with a fellow Hitchhiker who has your spiritual best interest at heart, you can be confident that when you leave the relative safety of the church to spend time with Wanderers and Nomads, you will return safely to the fold.

I hope by this point you're convinced that segregation from the unchurched is not only unhealthy for the sake of the kingdom, but that it's unbiblical as well. I also hope you recognize the dangers in excessive flocking, but also the realities of leaving the safety of the church to be with the unchurched. As Hitchhikers, God calls us to go out into the marketplace, the streets, the alleys, the roads, and the country lanes—in other words, everywhere the church is not—to reach the unreached. With that in mind, let's see how and where to meet and interact with those outside the faith.

What's ENOF?

By now you may be wondering about that "ENOF" stuff. I'm not a *Hooked on Phonics* failure, really, but I firmly believe every Hitchhiker needs to have ENOF: an **E**xpanding **N**etwork **O**f **F**riends.

While visiting a home fellowship group recently, one of their regular participants impressed me: a professional stand-up comedienne. This woman has a network of friends and acquaintances that reaches literally from coast to coast. I'd guess she can account for, and name, four or five hundred people she knows. Even more impressive, in my opinion, is the way she continually expands that network of friends through her comedy work and the ministry she does on the streets of Seattle where she occasionally appears as a street performer under a sign reading "Will Do Math for Money" (her day job is teaching high school math). She meets all sorts of interesting people and is intentional about building friendships with them.

However, I'm going to assume that most of you are a bit more like me—you have a rather finite circle of friends and acquaintances—and street performing isn't your thing. Malcolm Gladwell suggests that only about 3 percent of the population has an expansive network of connections—people they know by name.[3] The rest of us are, well, the rest of us. We have a limited circle of friends, which means we have probably already saturated these folks with invitations to church, conversations about God, and so on. If we're going to meet new people, two things have to be true. First, we have to be in proximity to people we don't yet know; and second, we have to make ourselves available to meet them.

Taking the Great Commission seriously means being in the proximity of people who are not already Christians. However, being in the same proximity as the unchurched isn't enough. Just because you go to a crowded mall filled with non-Christians doesn't mean you're expanding your friendship network. Obviously, you must make yourself available to meet someone. That means you're probably going to have to initiate a conversation.

Sound intimidating? For most of us it can be. The thought of heading to the mall to start conversations with complete strangers is enough to scare the wits out of most people. But that's not what this chapter is all about. Cold-call evangelism is a calling, not an expectation. We're not even talking about going to the mall! Those of you struck with panic can relax. This stuff is easy and anxiety-free, at least when you're doing it as Hitchhiker's Evangelism.

Can You Get ENOF?

Want to meet people who like to do what you like to do—people you have something in common with? Then combine ENOF with your hobbies, your leisure activities, and your ministries. The only change you'll have to make is to find a different playing field, somewhere with more than your current friends and somewhere with a dearth of Christians. There's not a reason in the world you can't get an Expanding Network Of Friends.

So what kind of hobbies do you already have? Do you golf? Quilt? Fish? Collect coins, stamps, or baseball cards? Oil, water, or tole paint? How about your leisure activities? Are you a taxi-driving mom or dad, driving your children from one activity to the next? Do you do dinner parties? Go to the movies? Meet your friends for a latté at the coffee shop? Take classes in bird watching or upholstery? And your ministries: Are you on a church committee? Serving as a deacon? Helping out at the interchurch food bank or homeless shelter?

You can use many hobbies, activities, and ministries to get ENOF. I'll elaborate a bit on a few of them in a moment. However, a lot of folks simply don't do much of that stuff. They're stay-at-home people. If you'd rather be at home than almost anywhere else, you're not alone. "Home" is probably the number one hang out for Christian adults. Cocooning, or staying at home, is almost certainly the real national pastime.

We have many reasons to seek the solace and safety of our homes, especially in our hustle-bustle world. I agree that we all need to take time for respite and recuperation. However, Hitchhikers are meant to be faring, an Old English word that literally means *to be in motion*, to be hitchhiking on the Way. Jesus put it like this: "The wind blows wherever it pleases. You hear its sound, but you cannot tell where it comes from or where it is going. So it is with everyone who is born of the Spirit" (Jn. 3:8). Note that the Spirit isn't in motion; we are. We're traveling wherever the Spirit takes us, and we're going somewhere—whether we're working, doing "church work," or playing.

Unfortunately, the only wayfaring some of us do is making our way home to dinner and TV. Again, Jesus has something to say about this: "Foxes have holes and birds have nests, but the Son of Man has no place to lay his head" (Mt. 8:20, TNIV). In other words, if we're going to be Hitchhikers hitchhiking through life with Jesus, we might not have as much time to hang out at the house. On the other hand, we may discover that blowing wherever the Spirit takes us is an adventure we wouldn't trade for all nine seasons of *Seinfeld's* reruns.

Develop ENOF Activities

Let's look at some ideas on how you can develop an Expanding Network Of Friends through your activities. However, as we look at these ideas, keep your eyes focused on the goal: to make new friends of the Wanderers and Nomads and to experience an opportunity to share your faith.

Step 1: Evaluate what you're already doing. Begin by making a list, mental or written, of all the regular activities you're doing now. List things like going to church, meeting with your friends on Tuesdays for coffee, taking the kids to basketball practice, going to the Bible study on Saturday mornings, seeing a movie, attending church meetings, lifting weights or doing aerobics at the gym, staying in and watching DVDs, and so on.

Now, take a look at that list. First, how many of these activities are you doing with Christian friends and/or church folk? If most of what you're doing is with Christians, and if you're serious about faithful Wayfaring, you'll have to make some decisions about what is necessary and what is nice. I always put church meetings on top of my suspect list: I've been on too many committees that talk about ministry but actually achieve very little. I suppose which curriculum to use for Vacation Bible School is important, but the church doesn't need lengthy discussions about it—church members should be able to trust whoever's in charge of VBS this year to make those decisions with their team. Let them make the decision while we get busy in going to all the world. Yes, if the water heater's broken and needs to be fixed, someone needs to make the decision to fix it. That's what the property committee is for; whoever is in charge of the property can call a plumber. They don't need our input because we should be able to trust the property chair (and if we can't, then our integrity demands we either reconsider why that person remains in charge or why we're still attending that particular church). Instead of going to church meeting after church meeting, today I go have a cup of coffee with my unchurched neighbor and see if Opportunity knocks. Though it might be a nice gesture to serve on a church committee; if we're brutally honest, most of the time a single leader can make most of the necessary decisions without everyone's input. We have to learn how to trust our leaders and allow them make their decisions while we go on to achieve the necessities of Hitchhiker's Evangelism. Too many of our churches today have more people sidelined on committee benches than they have on the evangelism playing field.

Use the same ruthless logic on every activity that involves other Christians. As a professor of mine was fond of saying, "You'll spend eternity with the saints—get out of the church and do some good." Weigh each activity against the mandate to make disciples. In some cases, you'll choose the side of spending time with your Christian friends. For instance, I seldom give up my weekly home fellowship for any other activity. It's too important to my Christian growth. I virtually never miss my weekly appointment with the spiritual friend who holds me accountable. On the other hand, I have cancelled longtime coffee and lunch meetings with fellow Christians to spend time in the places where I can rub shoulders with Wanderers and Nomads.

After you've crossed off some of your Christian activities, take a look at the rest of your list. You probably can't hang up your chauffeur's hat if you're in charge of getting the kids to ballet, but take a moment to consider carpooling. If you share the driving with one other parent, you've just halved your responsibility and can put that time to a more productive activity (although I'll share how to maximize your taxi time in a moment). With each of the activities on your list consider whether it's offering you an ENOF opportunity or not. You may not have to eliminate your gym time just because it doesn't put you into the proximity of the unchurched; you may simply need to find a different time to go or perhaps a different gym to work out in.

Again, weigh each activity against its potential to provide an opportunity to expand your friendship network. If the prospects aren't good, consider dropping the activity or finding a way to maximize the possibilities (see Step 2).

Step 2: Drop relationship-limiting activities. Once you've evaluated what you're already doing, the next step is to quit some of those activities that keep you from meeting and making new friends—especially unchurched friends. Now, I realize this is probably easier said than done. How do you say to your pastor, "Well Rev., just called to say I'm quitting the worship planning committee because I want to spend more time with non-Christians."? The solution is to be clear about what you're trying to accomplish. You should have no shame, and no detailed explanation should be necessary, to forego committees for the sake of the Great Commission.

Backing out of regular habits, appointments, and even obligations may not be easy; but if you're going to be a faithful Hitchhiker, it's probably going to be a necessity. In some cases, especially with fellow Hitchhikers, you may be able to explain that you're going to be spending the time doing evangelism. For others who may not understand the necessity for evangelism, you may want to gift them with a copy of this book rather than trying to convince them of the Great Commission's validity. Frankly, some aren't going to understand and never may. They'll take your departure as an intentional affront, and you can do nothing about it. The kindest thing you can do is to say you're sorry that their feelings were hurt and then rest in the knowledge that you're in good company—this is the kind of response Jesus promised his disciples would experience.

Step 3: Maximize Your Current Activities. Go back to the list you made in Step 1. Some of your activities likely have the potential to expand your unchurched friendship network. You're already in the proximity of Wanderers and Nomads. Now you simply need to maximize your availability.

Maximizing your availability means opening the gate so opportunity can come knocking. Although you've already read some ways to do this, the bottom line is that to make new friends you will probably have to reach out and start a conversation. Chapter 3 outlines how to carry a conversation, but let me suggest a few ways to make it even easier:

Ask for help. If you're engaged in a hobby (golf, scrapbooking, etc.) or any activity that requires some expertise, ask someone with more experience for help or advice. (My wife recently established a new ENOF friendship with the golf pro at our local golf course.)

Offer a compliment. No matter where you are or what you're doing, you can always find a way to compliment somebody.

Comment on the activity. This is especially effective if you're a taxi mom or dad for group activities. As you watch the kids play soccer, swim, dance, or create, offer positive comments or ask pertinent questions of the other parents/taxi drivers: "Is that your son? Wow, he sure does try hard!" and so on.

A second consideration when maximizing your activities is to make the most of the time. For the most part, this means training yourself to be alert to what's going on around you, especially learning to notice what others are doing in your near proximity. For someone like me, who happens to have ADHD and pretty much sees everything going on around me no matter what, this paragraph is hardly necessary. On the other hand, my wife has to make a conscious attempt to be aware of those around her—she gets involved in an activity and tunes out the world. For instance, if you're in an art class and everyone is painting a still life, you may well focus only on what you're doing. If you do, you'll miss the opportunity to compliment the student next to you or to make a pertinent comment about the muted lighting, and so on.

Finally, if you're serious about maximizing your activities, pursue your activities at the optimum times. For instance, if I want to meet new people, going to my local Starbucks at eight o'clock in the evening is virtually pointless because almost nobody hangs out there that late—they get their lattés and go. So, I do my coffee time in the mornings because I've learned that's the best window for meeting new people. Thus, if you find more opportunities to meet Wanderers and Nomads at the gym at six in the evening, then consider going then instead of first thing in the morning.

Add ENOF Activities

A lot of churched folk don't have any unchurched friends—and when I've chatted about that issue, many have confided they simply don't know where to meet the unchurched. And so, I close this chapter with a short litany of activities and ideas that I hope will serve to spark your imagination and to give you a place to start developing your own Expanding Network Of Friends.

- If you're involved in a Christian outreach ministry, such as an inter-church food bank, volunteer at a similar ministry that is unrelated to the faith (remember, your presence will make it a Christian service opportunity).

- Get involved in a club, such as Toastmasters, the Lions, the Optimists, or Rotary.
- Take a continuing education class, or pursue a degree at your local community college.
- Take up a new hobby, and join a related hobby club in your area.
- Volunteer almost anywhere except at a Christian ministry.
- Take group dance lessons (or group lessons on ceramics, cooking, photography, painting, etc.).
- Join or start a Neighborhood Watch group.
- Hang out at a bookstore, coffee shop, library, pub, or on a college campus enough to become a regular.

The only way the Great Commission is ever going to be realized is if we become Saint Georges who are willing to do battle with the dragon of Christian segregation. Yes, racism is still a nasty beast that still haunts society, but the longer we remain self-focused, the smaller the effect of the faith on our world and evils such as racism. It may not be easy for you to loosen the ties you have with your local church, but the Kingdom of God rests in your hands. People like you must be willing to say "Enough!" to church to create ENOF for the Great Commission.

By the Way Reflections

1. Have you seen the dragon of Christian segregation at work in your congregation? How? What do you think can be done to slay the dragon?
2. What church support activities are you involved in? How many of these activities would cease to function completely if you were relocated out of state next week? What would happen if they did cease to function?
3. What faith-based ministries is your church involved with that are duplicated in your community by a secular organization? What do you think the effect would be if the church got involved in the secular organization instead?
4. How many unchurched friendships have you developed in the last year?
5. Make a list of the activities available in your community that could facilitate meeting Wanderers and Nomads. Which of these activities will you get involved with this year to expand your network of unchurched friends?

NOTES

[1]"2004 American Community Survey: Data Profile Highlights," *US Census Bureau,* http://factfinder.census.gov/servlet/ACSSAFFFacts?_event=&geo_id=01000US&_ geoContext=01000US&_street=&_county=&_cityTown=&_state=&_zip=&_lang=en&_ sse=on&ActiveGeoDiv=&_useEV=&pctxt=fph&pgsl=010.

[2]Jerry Sullivan, "The Passenger Pigeon: Once There Were Billions," in *Hunting for Frogs on Elston, and Other Tales from Field and Street* (Chicago: Chicago University Press, 2004), http://www.press.uchicago.edu/Misc/Chicago/779939pass.html.

[3]Malcolm Gladwell, *The Tipping Point: How Little Things Can Make a Big Difference* (New York: Little, Brown & Co., 2002), 41.

CHAPTER SIX

Faith at Home

When Jesus saw this, he was indignant. He said to them, "Let the little children come to me, and do not hinder them, for the kingdom of God belongs to such as these. Truly I tell you, anyone who will not receive the kingdom of God like a little child will never enter it." (Mk. 10:14–15)

Some things are painful to write—this chapter is one of them. You see, I believe that home is the one place in the world where a Hitchhiker's child ought to always feel the protection of God, the compassion of Jesus, and the empowerment of the Holy Spirit. Home should be more of a sanctuary for the embattled than a church building could ever dream of being. It should exude the holiness of the finest cathedrals, but with the peace and tranquility of a monastic cloister. Home should be a safe place for the family to explore faith, to ask questions, to wrestle with doubts, and to triumphantly emerge as fully committed disciples of Jesus. That's what home should be.

Many pastors experience a seemingly ever-expanding chasm between *should* and *is*. Some of the settings where my wife and I served were transitional churches; home for our family was sometimes more like a bomb shelter where wide-eyed, frightened children watched their overwhelmed parents cope with the aftermath of adversarial church meetings and contentious church bullies. In one case, the church parking lot was in front of our house. From their bedroom our children could hear the loud post-board meetings taking place out there until hours after their mother the pastor had returned home. Home was the place where triage was the norm—whoever had the worst wounds got the primary care. With five children, our home could look like the sitcom *M*A*S*H** just after the choppers arrived, except we had no studio audience and nobody was laughing.

In that environment we struggled with trying to nurture our children's spirituality. Indeed, I must confess I found it hard enough to nurture our own spirituality, let alone give much attention to our children's (something else we weren't taught in seminary). The task wasn't easy, and we seldom felt like we succeeded. Still, today, all of our children have found, or are finding, their spiritual footing and are engaged in a variety of faith settings—not because we're such great parents and models, but because God's been especially gracious and they have had some positive experiences within the walls of the church.

Apparently, my wife and I aren't the only ones who struggle with the issue of faith in the home. Raising children in the faith is difficult for many, if not most, Christians. So many distractions and detractors rise from the church and from Christianity itself. Even though 77 percent of people in the United States claim to be Christian,[1] indications suggest that a striking minority of us are making the practice of our Way-faring a top priority in our lives. A recent survey revealed that 85 percent of Christians admitted faith wasn't their top priority.[2] If faithful Way-faring isn't a serious priority in our lives, the likelihood of our children staying with the faith decreases significantly. Besides, if we're not demonstrating our faith in every area of our lives, by the time our children are teenagers they'll likely either conclude our religion is inauthentic or else adopt a version of Christianity that is something less than life transforming.

Houston, Seattle, New York, Galesburg, Prosser...
We Have a Problem

Why is it so difficult to embed a lasting Christian faith in our kids? What keeps so many of us from sharing our faith journey with them? Once upon a time in North America people believed that if you faithfully took your children with you to church, they wouldn't even miss a beat even through high school and college—they'd attend a church of the same brand name as the one they grew up in. Not so anymore! Repeatedly, I've heard pastors and researchers cite the same sad statistic: churched kids drop out of the church, and all too often the faith, between junior high and college. Many of us have clung to the verse: "Start children off on the way they should go, and even when they are old they will not turn from it" (Prov. 22:6), but the past couple of generations' statistics don't reflect that universal hope. The number of Christians continues to slide. The church is experiencing what can be described only as a mass exodus. No matter what city, town, or village in the United States or Canada you happen to live in, you've got a problem.

The Proximity Factor

You may remember that in chapter 4 I spoke of the proximity factor—that in your work life you'll spend 90,000 hours or so with coworkers who will scrutinize how your faith impacts your life. In other words, for eight hours a day it's vitally important to live your faith faithfully. For many, the implications of that insight is that you can let your hair down when you get home.

If you think you're under scrutiny at work, that's nothing compared to the microscope you're under at home. The average child will spend over 140,000 hours at home by the time they're eighteen. If you work full time, you get a break—they'll observe your Way-faring only 119,000 hours before they leave home.

By the time your children are twelve-years-old or so—a mere 80,000 hours in your proximity—they've discovered that you're not perfect and that you don't know everything. They know whether or not your faith is for real, for show, or for naught. Kids at that age have become well acquainted, and often a bit jaded, with talk that doesn't walk. As parents, we know we're not perfect, that we don't know everything, and that our actions don't always reflect the well-intentioned words we say. Still, we often get the impression that our children expect otherwise.

Of course, all this holds true if you're married and your true love isn't a believer, except that in a marriage proximity takes on additional dimensions. Marriage creates an intimacy and a transparency that reveals some of our deepest "stuff." Your spouse knows things about you that you may pray never reaches the ears of another. But more importantly, your spouse is a long-term witness to whether or not your faith is an influence to your behavior beyond the public forum. They've seen your real faith in action in the bedroom, when you have a disagreement, when you're in a foul mood, or when they're in a foul mood.

No matter who we are or how "good" we may try to be, our imperfect example gets in the way of communicating our faith to those we are closest to. All too often our faith can't stand up to the proximity factor.

Midlife Conversions

Some of you reading this book came to the faith later in life or have a spouse who did. If you're one of these, those closest to you can testify to the before and the after. For some, their commitment to Jesus has so totally transformed their lives that they exemplify Paul's statement "Therefore, if anyone is in Christ, he is a new creation; the old has gone, the new has come!" (2 Cor. 5:17). Others, however, have lifelong habits, behaviors, and even addictions they have to contend with. Though the transformation of the spirit is real, it may be some time before others see an all-new you.

Whether the transformation is instant or ongoing, the family remembers. They recall the less-than-savory moments: promises made and promises broken; hurtful looks, words, and deeds; and every bad habit that's still left to shake.

Jesus experienced something akin to this dilemma when he visited the synagogue in his hometown of Nazareth and began to teach. Though they were impressed with what he had to say, everyone remembered the younger, unremarkable Jesus, the son of the local carpenter. They simply couldn't believe this kid was anything more than that (Mt. 13:54–58).

A commitment to Jesus and our immersion into the faith changes lives; however, our past has been indelibly etched into the minds and hearts of our family members. They remember yesterday's yesterday all the way back, so their skepticism about our new life is deeply rooted and the ability to effectively share our faith may be hindered.

The Pastor's Paradox

What can a pastor say about PKs (Preacher's Kids)? The stereotype pictures preacher's kids as rebellious, obnoxious, and almost always to blame for whatever goes awry at the youth group. Let me set the record straight: That stereotype is an unfair characterization of the children raised in the parsonage, and sometimes it's even undeserving.

On the other hand, who could blame preacher's kids for being a bit on the wild side? They know the truth about their parents and society's assumption that they live in some sort of a perpetual state of holiness—after all, God chose and called them just like Moses, Samuel, Jeremiah, and Isaiah. But PKs know better. They've been in the car while mom and dad argue right up to the church parking lot and then leave the car with smiles on their faces and "love" in their hearts. PKs know that their parents aren't perfect, that they don't know everything, and that no matter how real and how deep their faith may be, it doesn't always translate into love, joy, peace, patience, kindness, goodness, faithfulness, gentleness, and self-control.

It's one thing to be a professing Christian and to be under the microscope. It's something else entirely to be a clergy parent. The expectations of church and society on the clergy family are high and the pressure to conform higher yet. In time, PKs often come to resent the pressure. Then they either rebel in ways everyone can see, or they rebel by silently crossing their arms, closing their minds, and rejecting the expectations, the church, and even the faith outright. Either way, effectively sharing the faith within a pastor's family can be a daunting and difficult task.

This chapter is meant for more than just pastor-parents. Instilling a lasting faith in any family is difficult for many reasons. We're going to leave the nitty-gritty of why it's a problem to someone else's research project. We want to take a look at how we can effectively create an environment where faith can be cultivated, planted, and nurtured to maturity in our homes.

What You See Is What You Get: Integrity at Home

An aphorism complains, "I can't hear what you're saying because your actions are speaking so loudly!" Sadly, our behaviors regularly don't match the ideal of living a faith-filled and faith-controlled life. Nobody's perfect! Though we try to be as Christlike as possible, we not only fall short of Christianity's ideals, we fall short of our family's expectations.

The obvious solution would be to simply become, in the words of Mary Poppins, "Practically perfect in every way." But that isn't likely to happen for any of us anytime soon. We really have only one other choice: We have to integrate our faith with the way we live. The saying "Christians aren't perfect, but they are forgiven" is true, even though the slogan has been abused as an excuse for bad behavior. No one in your family over the age of twelve actually expects you to be perfect, but they do expect you to be a model Hitchhiker who has integrated faith with behavior.

Being a faithful spiritual model in your own home is not an easy task for even the most practiced and mature Hitchhiker. But it is possible. You won't become practically perfect overnight, but you can learn to walk the walk of the faithful in short order if you'll take it one step at a time. And the first step every believer has to take is to get milk.

Get Milk

Milk is the staple of life for newborn babies, both in the crib and in the church. The milk delivered from the church doesn't come in a bottle—everyone knows that. On the other hand, many believe that the spiritual milk that nourishes baby Christians comes directly from the Bible. Oh, that this were true! The Bible is a rich resource for the faith, but let's take just a moment to reflect on the early church. During the first two centuries, the church multiplied new Christians so rapidly that the movement exponentially grew from its humble beginning of 120 (Acts 1:15) to many, many thousands of believers from the Middle East to Africa, throughout Asia, and into Europe. But here's the mystery: They did all that without a single copy of the Bible.[3]

Christian education today is primarily about teaching the foundation of the Christian faith by turning to the Bible, both Old and New Testaments. We learn about Adam and Abraham and David and Jesus and Paul. We learn the stories of Eden, the great flood, the exodus, the slaying of Goliath, the rise and fall of Jerusalem, the birth of Jesus, the crucifixion, and the apocalypse to come. All that's important stuff to know—it is the foundation of the faith. However, when the New Testament writers wrote letters to the Hitchhikers, they seldom recounted any of that. Paul virtually never referred to Old Testament stories, and only rarely to New Testament stories, when he wrote to non-Jewish believers.

When the early church referred to spiritual milk, they weren't primarily interested in imparting education. On the other hand, they were very interested in training new Christians to travel the Way faithfully. In other words, drinking the church's spiritual milk grew strong spiritual bodies that could walk the walk, not just talk the talk.

The writer of Hebrews sums up the "formula" for spiritual milk:

> In fact, though by this time you ought to be teachers, you need someone to teach you the elementary truths of God's word all over again. You need milk, not solid food! …Therefore let us move beyond the elementary teachings about Christ and be taken forward to maturity, not laying again the foundation of repentance from acts that lead to death, and of faith in God, instruction about cleansing rites, the laying on of hands, the resurrection of the dead, and eternal judgment. And God permitting, we will do so. (Heb. 5:12, 6:1–3, TNIV)

Milk isn't learning a great deal of information; it's putting a little information into a great deal of practice. "Repentance from acts that lead to death" and "faith in God" are about what you do, not about what you know.

The problem is, most North American Christians are educated beyond their obedience. Correcting that deficit isn't going to happen overnight, and it isn't going to happen at all as long as the church continues to emphasize education over training. In other words, if you're going to get milk, you're going to have to take responsibility for getting it on your own.

Like an ingredient list on food packaging labels, the primary and most important ingredients in spiritual milk's formula are listed first: repentance and faith. Often we think of repentance as being a mental exercise, but that's not the way the New Testament church defined it. Repentance was a behavioral change, not simply an admission of guilt. By the end of the first century, when someone became a new believer they entered a training program that lasted up to three years. During that time they were trained to become a Christian and taught to put their faith into practice in their daily lives. Indeed, *The Apostolic Traditions of Hippolytus of Rome*, one of the earliest teachings on the subject, dated at about A.D. 215, sheds some light on just how important behavioral change was to the early church. In chapter 17:1–2 it teaches that new believers "will hear the word for three years. Yet if someone is earnest and perseveres well in the matter, it is not the time that is judged, but the conduct."[4] In other words, how well the new believer fares on the Way makes the difference. Being a "doer" of the word is the key to getting milk and growing strong, healthy spiritual bodies.

Repentance and faith are both action words. Repentance means to turn from one way of living to embrace another. For Hitchhikers, it means putting an end to the bad habits and the less-than-savory behaviors we've practiced for so long and replacing them with faithful Way-faring alternatives. Faith means to trust, which is more than assenting to the facts of the faith. For Hitchhikers, faith means letting God be in control of even the most mundane decisions of our lives. Easier said than done? Of course it is. But that's why you need help.

Get Help

Becoming an integrated model who walks the talk even at home is not a journey to be taken alone. For one, it's a rough, rocky, and very narrow path. If you haven't roped yourself to an experienced Hitchhiker, with every misstep you'll slide over the edge. That's where most North American believers find themselves, and they spend most of their lives trying to scramble back onto the trail. Many of those who slip end up battered, bruised, and broken on the rocks below. They may never rise to try again. Others cling to the edge of the path and call for help, but too often those on the path above them are so focused on keeping their own balance that they can't hear the pleas. The only safe and sure way to travel the Way is to do so with someone who will share the journey with you. After all, isn't that what Hitchhiking is all about?

Now, I know that it's not in our American nature to ask for help. We're an independent people who take a lot of pride in self-reliance. But, in the words of Ecclesiastes "Two are better than one…If one falls down, his friend can help him up. But pity the man who falls and has no one to help him up!" (Eccl. 4:9–10). Way-faring, like any dangerous undertaking, is not a solo adventure—that's why Jesus always sent his disciples out two by two.

I briefly referred to Journey Groups in chapter 5. In my books *House Church Manual* and *High-Voltage Spirituality*,[5] I fully explain Journey Group Partnerships, but let me briefly introduce the process here. A Journey Group Partner is someone who is willing to help you become the model Hitchhiker you were created to be by holding you accountable for your behaviors.

Before talking more about the Journey Groups, let me first say that *accountability* is perhaps the most frightening word in the language of the church, next only to the word *confession.* However, both accountability and confession are the core practices of Way-faring companionships.

Already I can feel your stress levels rising as visions of wagging fingers, shaking heads, or curtained confessionals flash through your mind. Never fear! I promise the security of being roped to a traveling companion, as well as the distance you will travel on the Way, will far outweigh your fears of the moment. Allow me to explain.

When Way-faring, being accountable doesn't mean you're giving permission for someone to judge you, to correct you, or to chastise you when you slip. Instead, in a Way-faring companionship, accountability means giving yourself permission to be honest with someone willing to listen without comment or critique.

In a Way-faring companionship, accountability is a shared experience. Traveling the narrow Way is safest when the two of you are roped together, meaning your companion is as tied to you as you are to your companion. As such, it's a two-way street; when you agree to travel together you will hold your partner as accountable as he or she holds you. Like your partner, you will not have permission to judge, correct, chastise, comment, or critique. Your companion is only giving you permission to listen. Nothing more, nothing less.

If the word *accountability* comes with baggage, *confession* is laden with a steamer ship's cargo. With the advent of the Protestant Reformation, the practice of confession fell into disrepute, never mind that it remains an expected practice for faithful Hitchhikers (Jas. 5:16; 1 Jn. 1:9). The problems with confession arose when the clergy determined that they were in charge of pronouncing absolution (forgiveness). Over time, this led to the rites of penance, which is a nice way of saying the clergy started doling out punishment. Some even went so far as offering forgiveness at a price: make a donation, get guaranteed absolution. Though a big part of repentance is making things right with those we've wronged, neither punishment nor money can take the place of reconciliation.

All that's to say that if we're going to get the spiritual milk we need to grow into model Hitchhikers that even our twelve-year-old can look up to, we need a Way-faring companion we can be—and will be—accountable to.

Traveling with a Journey Group Partner

Nothing is like traveling with a Journey Group Partner. It's nearly impossible to enjoy the view along the Way when you trip, slip, and stumble with every step you try to take. Traveling the Way with a companion, however, changes everything. From gingerly trying to navigate the Way step-by-step, you'll soon be making bold strides as your Christian life turns from talking the walk to confidently walking the talk.

It all begins with your Journey Group Partner. Your traveling companion should be the same gender as you are. Some issues that come up in a Journey Group are inappropriate to share with someone of the opposite gender. This, of course, precludes your spouse from becoming your Journey Group Partner. I often get resistance on this issue, but the reason for the rule is simple: Every marriage has times when it would be unhealthy and unwise to fully disclose our present thoughts or feelings to our spouse.

Your traveling companion must be both available and accessible. A Journey Group Partnership requires about a half-hour each week for a one-on-one get-together. You can meet over coffee or lunch or while you commute to work together, but the face-to-face is a critical component of safe and integrity-filled Way-faring.

The only agenda for your weekly get-together is to read and answer the eleven accountability questions on the next page and to answer them in turn. You'll notice that question number nine is blank so you can be held accountable for an issue that may not be on the list. For instance, mine is, "Have you put off an important task that you need to accomplish?" You'll also notice that with the exception of question number six you will have no need to elaborate or explain any of your answers. Let your yes be yes and your no be no. You can offer an explanation, ask for advice, or discuss the issue if you would like; however, just because you decide to open up and bare your soul, don't expect your partner to do the same. They will if they want to; they won't if they don't.

The genius behind these accountability questions is that they cover virtually every issue in our lives. As you engage the process with your traveling companion and get honest with your behaviors, you'll find your walk will become more consistent with your talk—which will make a good impression even on your twelve-year-old.

Unfortunately, it takes time for this spiritual milk to transform us. While you're growing, you will make mistakes. Old habits will rear their heads, thoughtless words and inconsiderate deeds will slip out, and your family may take the brunt of your sin. The model you are won't be the model you want to be. The only faithful recourse you have in times like these is to get real.

The Accountability Questions

1. Have you been a testimony this week to the greatness of Jesus Christ with both your words and actions?

2. Have you been exposed to sexually alluring material or allowed your mind to entertain inappropriate sexual thoughts about another this week?

3. Have you lacked integrity in your financial dealings or coveted something that does not belong to you?

4. Have you been honoring, understanding, and generous in your important relationships this week?

5. Have you damaged another person by your words either behind his or her back or face to face?

6. Have you given in to an addictive behavior this past week? Explain.

7. Have you continued to remain angry toward another?

8. Have you secretly wished for another's misfortune?

9. (*Your Personalized Accountability Question?*)————————

10. Did you faithfully read the Bible this week and did you hear from God? What are you going to do about it?

11. Have you been completely honest with me?

Get Real

Getting real is what transforms our missteps along the Way into model Way-faring. Getting real is also one of the most difficult practices of all because it necessitates not only taking responsibility for our words and actions, but admitting them and making amends for them.

We live in a cultural climate of pass-the-buck. We all seem to be victims, and anyone or everyone else is to blame. God-forbid, when something is our fault, that we take responsibility. Instead, we have a tendency to cover it up or to proffer lame excuses. That's not the way of a Hitchhiker. Hitchhikers don't just take responsibility. They also humbly admit their faults and foibles and are more interested in receiving forgiveness than in being understood. Perhaps most importantly, they're committed to behaving differently. Many people promise to try to do better, but Hitchhikers do more than just try. They are doing something about it by being real, by making amends, and by engaging in an accountability partnership (such as a Journey Group). Being real involves more than saying, "I'm sorry."

Six steps lead to getting real. For a change, the first step tends to be the easiest.

Step 1: Recognize when you're falling short. This step is generally the easiest because Hitchhikers are almost always painfully aware when we do or say something that hurts another. However, there's more to this than just entertaining a passing thought of "Oh, that wasn't very nice of me." When we recognize we've fallen short, especially if we're mid-sentence or mid-deed, we must learn to immediately engage step 2.

Step 2: Stop it! This step isn't so easy because once we've started something (or are responding to something), putting the brakes on is like trying to stop a rolling locomotive. Nonetheless, this is an important step to learn. The more we practice it, the less likely we are to repeat the same offense, so when that ugly word leaves your mouth, stop right there and move on to step 3.

Step 3: Humbly take responsibility. Note the word *humbly*. I'm using that word in the purest and most gentle form I know. You humbly take responsibility by taking a step back and immediately taking responsibility for your deed: "I shouldn't have said that; I was wrong" or "I shouldn't have done that; I was wrong." No reasons, no excuses, simply, "I shouldn't have _____; I was wrong."

Step 4: Make amends. Now. We often think that the biblical system of justice is punishment. That's not the case. In every circumstance where a sin is committed against someone, the demanded response is an attempt at restoration, not punishment. The goal was to put things right. Thieves were to return what they stole with interest. Whatever wrong was done, the consequence was to make it as undone as possible. That's the point of making amends—to undo as much as possible what you've done, and to do it right now. Putting off making amends may intensify the hurt or damage our thoughtlessness caused. Sometimes making something right is as easy as apologizing and conceding a point you may have been vehemently defending in an argument. At other times it may be much more costly. What it takes to make amends, however, is dependent on what the wronged person needs to make it right. You can't make this decision based on what seems logical to you. Remember, you hurt them, and you have to make it right with them.[6]

Step 5: Commit to do better. Being real and building integrity with your family depends on your commitment and follow-through as a faithful Hitchhiker. Once you've made it right with them, make a commitment to do better from then on. But don't just leave it at that, tell them how you're going to do better. If you were late for an important family event, tell them what you will do to be on time from then on (and then follow through and do it). If you spoke harshly, tell them how you will learn to be more gentle and genteel when you have a disagreement. Only after you've taken responsibility for your deeds, made amends, and committed to doing better are you ready for the last step.

Step 6: Ask forgiveness. It's not easy to look at your six-year-old and ask forgiveness. It's even more difficult to ask forgiveness of your fifteen-year-old. Asking forgiveness of your spouse can be formidable. However, only when you seek forgiveness do you learn the depth of damage you've done. Asking for forgiveness is a humbling experience and transcends what we typically call an apology. "I'm sorry" is not asking forgiveness. "I apologize" is not asking for forgiveness. Only, "Will you forgive me?" qualifies as asking for forgiveness. Forgiveness is an act that comes from beyond yourself. If you've come this far in the process, I hope you've seen the hurt you've caused and you have a contrite heart that's filled with remorse. Once you've been there and truly regret your misdeed, only then are you ready to seek forgiveness.

Forgiveness isn't guaranteed just because you ask for it. Depending on the depth of the hurt, your family may not be ready to forgive and to be fully reconciled. The only response you can faithfully make at that point is to try to understand their heart and to let things be. Forgiveness is an act of mercy and grace that must be freely given. Badgering someone for it; trying to guilt them into giving it; bargaining, threatening, or any response other than humble acceptance of reality is antithetical to traveling on the Way.

Learning to be real is one of the most important lessons in this book. Too many North American Christians practice the default cultural norms of blame shifting, responsibility avoiding, and lame excuses—all of which have only served to stain the name of the church, of the faith, and of Christ himself. Practice being real wherever you are to become the model Hitchhiker God created you to be in your home; indeed, especially put it into practice at home.

Home Faith Formation

As North Americans of the twenty-first century, virtually all of us have contributed to the prostitution of our institutions. The government largely exists to protect us from those who would seek to harm us, but we have pressed it into service as a purveyor of social services of all kinds: a morality-legislating institution, as well as a retirement investment firm. Our schools exist to educate our children, but we have demanded that they should also instill values, good manners, and respect for authority. The church exists to assail the gates of hell and rescue those imprisoned by the dark spiritual forces that ensnare and enslave the Wanderers. But we expect it to provide Christian education, discipleship, worship services, a Christian friendship network, pastoral counseling, social services for those inside and outside of the faith, membership services such as weddings and funerals, any evangelism that may need to be done, as well as instilling spiritual grounding and morality in our children. All that and I'm certain I've left some things out. With all of those expectations, the church has its hands full.

Using the Jewish Family Model

It hasn't always been that way. During the first few centuries of Christianity, the church used the Jewish family model for handing down the faith to the next generation. Parents received training from the church, and children were immersed in the faith by their parents. Read the following passage from Deuteronomy and imagine what your home life would look like if you modeled your faith in your family based on this passage:

> These are the commands, decrees and laws the LORD your God directed me to teach you…Impress them on your children. Talk about them when you sit at home and when you walk along the road, when you lie down and when you get up. Tie them as symbols on your hands and bind them on your foreheads. Write them on the doorframes of your houses and on your gates. (Deut. 6:1, 7–9)

Like their Jewish predecessors, the early Christians saw God's hand in everything. From the rising of the sun to the raisins on the table, God was acknowledged, thanked, and praised for every good gift. When life wasn't good or fair, they praised God that they were able to experience a taste of Jesus' suffering. They considered every act sacred. The Spirit was present and acknowledged at meals, at work, at the marketplace, and in the coliseum. The accounts of Jesus, the church, and the apostles were the topics of mealtime conversation, as well as after-dinner chats and bedtime stories.

In the fifth century, Saint Patrick embellished the Jewish family model and used it to introduce Christianity and change the face of Ireland forever. The Irish Christians not only saw God's hand in everything, they adorned their homes with Christian symbols to remind themselves they were in the presence of God. They incorporated ritual into their everyday lives to remind themselves to call upon the power of God. They took seriously the scriptural instructions to talk about the Lord when they sat at home, when they walked along the road, when they laid down at night, and when they got up in the morning.

The organized church was not charged with raising our children in the faith. We were. Far too often we abdicate our responsibility and leave it to the institution. That's not how it's supposed to be, nor how it has to be. You have no reason not to take the lead and reclaim the task, yea the privilege, of imparting faith to your family.

The remainder of this chapter presents a number of practices that will help you create an environment in your home that establishes and nurtures the foundations of the faith within the hearts and minds of the whole family. Some of the ideas will sound pretty basic. Others may sound radical, at least at first, but give each one a try for a month before you write it off. You may find the ones that seem the most preposterous are the practices that make the most difference in your family.

From the Cradle to the Grave

It's never too early or too late to create a home environment that's friendly to faith formation; however, the earlier you start, the better. A family that raises their child from infancy in a faith-filled home will have built a sound foundation in their child's life. On the other hand, if you have teenagers and this is your first attempt at establishing a faith-filled home, expect some push-back—a *lot* of push-back—as you try some of these ideas.

However, faith foundation is not just for children. Hitchhikers are travelers on the Way, not stationary moss gatherers. Unless we've graduated past "practically perfect in every way," we all have some growing to do. Don't discount these ideas just because you don't have children or you're older than you'd care to admit. Building a home where faith fills even the air you breathe is a worthy endeavor that will make a difference in your life and ultimately in the lives of your friends, relatives, acquaintances, neighbors, and coworkers.

Making Home Sacred: From the Front Door

If anyone takes the admonitions of Deuteronomy seriously, those of the Jewish faith do. From the mezuzah on the front doorpost to the candles kindled on Friday evening, their homes are sacred places of sanctuary and prayer. A Hitchhiker's home is both a refuge and place of prayer. Making your home sacred is a matter of décor, practice, and intentionality of heart.

Not just the religious symbols or worshipful practices make a home sacred. A home is sanctified when its space is dedicated to God and the Divine Presence is invited, recognized, and welcomed. If the Spirit of God is overlooked, the space might as well be a little house on the freeway for all the spiritual energy that will be experienced there. A Hitchhiker's home tends to be replete with symbols and practices to help call the mind into the spiritual reality of God. From the moment the sight of your home appears through the mist of morning, to the time your eyes (and your children's eyes) close at the end of the day, the sacred space you create in your home becomes the foundation for embedding the faith in your family's spirit.

A Candle in the Window

A very old custom in Christianity is the practice of having a lit candle in the front window of the home at night. The candle serves a number of purposes. First, it's a symbol that God's presence resides in your home. Second, it's a beacon that draws you to a safe harbor from the storms of life. Third, it's a proclamation that your home is a place of peace. Finally, it's an invitation to passersby that yours is a home of hospitality.

Written on Your Doorposts

The Jewish community took the command to write the law on their doorposts seriously so they created the mezuzah. A mezuzah consists of a small parchment with God's name *Shaddai* (the "Guardian of the doorways of Israel") and the text of Deuteronomy 6:4–9 and 11:13–21 written on it. The parchment is rolled up, placed into a small case, and then attached to the doorposts of Jewish homes to serve both as a reminder of God's watch and care over the household and as an act of obedience to scripture. In many homes, a mezuzah is attached to every doorway in the home, except for washrooms and small closets. Every time a resident passes through the doorway, they touch the mezuzah and then kiss the fingers that touched it as a sign of their love and devotion to the Divine.

Putting a sign of your faith on the doorposts of your home is an excellent way to get yourself into the habit of reminding yourself of God's presence. Mezuzot (plural for mezuzah) are available online, at synagogue bookstores, and in many other Jewish faith shops. Since the Bible teaches that God "grafted us into the roots" and adopted Christians into Israel, Hitchhikers can feel confident about putting a mezuzah on their doorposts. However, if you choose to put them on or in your home, be sure to learn how to properly affix the mezuzot to your doorposts (we've found that clerks in synagogue and Judaica shops are wonderfully open and helpful).

We can affix many other symbols to our doorposts as a reminder of the Lord's presence in our lives. Small crosses, crucifixes, Celtic knots, and anchors are just a few of the many choices you have available.[7] Choose one of these, or some other meaningful symbol, and attach it to your doorpost to serve as a reminder that you're entering the sacred sanctuary where God is at residence with you and your family.

Interior Decorating

You have almost endless options for decorating to help create sacred space within your home. A visit to any Christian gift shop can inspire your creative spirit with a multitude of ideas. From paintings to statuary, tapestries to candles, your creativity is limited only by your bank account.

Some of the most meaningful decorations and symbols, however, are the ones created by the hands of your family. For instance, I recently visited a home where I noticed their mantle sported a large decorated shoe box with a burning tea light in it. I stepped closer to see if there were some significance to the box and was surprised to find myself looking at an intricately decorated shrine. Pasted to the inside of the box was a collage of magazine pictures and headline words. The pictures were of Jesus, some of the saints, and sacred places from around the world. The headlines read words like praise, joy, God, forgive, and so on. Propped within the box behind the tea light were school photographs of a couple of children. I learned that these were local children who weren't Christians.

The family was praying for them. Indeed, the shrine had been made during a home worship service, and the whole family had a hand in its creation.

So many ideas are available for decorating your home in sacred objects d'art that even another book could barely hold them all.[8] However, look over the brief list below for ideas that could work in your home:

- Hang a faith-based painting, drawing, or relief.
- Display a cross and/or crucifix (my mother has a collection of crosses on her dining room wall).
- Keep a Christ-candle lit in the living room (a white pillar candle).
- Paint a mural or a religious-based border on your walls.
- Place a small religious sculpture or figurine on your mantle or on end tables.
- Display a paten and chalice (used in communion—my wife collects chalices and displays them on the mantle).
- Create a prayer wall by installing a corkboard and attaching prayer needs and answers to prayer.
- Have faith-based books and magazines available.
- Set aside and decorate part of a room for prayer—you could include a prayer mat or cushions, candles, incense, pictures of people you're praying for, a Bible, a journal, a prayer shawl, and so on.
- Use your refrigerator to display religious artwork by the children.
- Decorate your refrigerator with meaningful fridge magnets (they make nice gifts as people leave your home).
- Put word magnets (magnetic poetry) on your fridge and arrange them in prayers and praises.
- Buy or make icons for your walls.
- Decorate a wire tree or a "potted tree branch" with sacred symbols such as Chrismons (do a Google image search for Chrismons for examples).

Making Time Sacred

Once again, I want to refer to the Jewish faith as an example of making time sacred in the home. Before the advent of synagogues, faithful Israelites traveled to the temple three times each year for the feasts of Unleavened Bread (Passover), Weeks (Pentecost), and Tabernacles (Succoth). Other than these times, the typical Israelite trained their children in the faith at home. As we read in Deuteronomy, the parents evangelized their children by making God the topic of conversation from their rising to their lying down and all points in between. It's not that other topics of conversation weren't available to wile away the time; they could have spent their days talking about the crops, local news and gossip, the weather, and so on. Of course, they talked about these things during the day, but Israelite parents were intentional about turning the conversation to God whenever they saw the hand of the Divine intervening in their lives. They saw God in virtually everything, so keeping the topic alive wasn't all that difficult.

As Hitchhikers we aren't so disciplined, nor do we tend to see God so prevalently in our lives. We far too easily dismiss the rising of the sun as a phenomenon of nature and science rather than to recall that God is the Lord over both nature *and* science. The same goes for the food we set on our table to the comfort of the furnace that keeps us warm—God's hand is in it all, we just don't recognize it anymore.

This problem has a two-part solution. First, to see the Divine in everything around us, we have to make time sacred. Until we're sensitized, we can't impart the mystery of the spiritual realm to anyone else, not even our children. Learning to be sensitive, however, takes practice and will likely feel awkward at first. Rest assured, however, that as you routinely integrate these suggestions into your everyday life, you'll build habits and traditions that will sensitize you to the presence of God. The second part of the solution is to become intentional in making and sharing sacred time with the rest of the family. As you embark on this leg of the journey, as you put into practice seeing God's hand in your life, your children's spiritual eyes will begin to open to the wonders that the Spirit has for all who seek.

Making Mealtimes Sacred

Once upon a time, the family ate breakfast, lunch, and dinner together (or breakfast, dinner, and supper, depending on where you were raised). As families left agriculture and family-owned and operated businesses, the midday meal was dropped from the repertoire. Today, it's a rare family who gathers around the dinner table more than once or twice a week. Even rarer is a family who eats breakfast together.

Traditionally, mealtimes are marked as sacred times. So many important and sacred events happen around meals in the Bible. Abraham prepared a meal for the angels of God. All of the ancient Israelite festivals involve feasting or fasting. Elisha miraculously fed a hundred men with a few loaves. Jesus fed 4,000 and later 5,000. When he resurrected Jairus's daughter, he told the family to feed her. Zacchaeus invited his tax collecting friends to a banquet he threw for Jesus. Of course, the Last

Supper is the most sacred meal any of us will share this side of eternity. Meals are sacred time opportunities.

You can make your mealtime sacred in a number of ways. Begin by turning off the television, the cell phones, and the stereo. At the beginning of the Sabbath meal, the mother "kindles the Sabbath candles" by lighting at least two candles, reciting a prayer welcoming the sacred time, and offering prayers for her family. This marks the mealtime as a sacred event. Today, some Christians continue the practice of lighting the candles with a blessing such as this:

> Blessed are you, Lord Our God, Ruler of the universe,
> Who sanctified us by your word,
> and commanded us to be a light to the nations
> and who gave us Jesus Our Messiah, the Light of the world.

Others mark the time as sacred by saying a simple grace before the meal. If you already say grace at meals, using that prayer to introduce sacred time may not be effective because it has probably come to be known as the starting point for eating rather than dedicating the time to God. However, if your family isn't used to saying grace, or if you're committed to using grace as the mark of sacred time, offer a prayer that is more than just gratitude for the food, but indicates that the time around the table belongs to God.

In many families, dinnertime is a hodgepodge of conversation about the day: What happened at school or at work? What's the latest news on…? Did you hear that…? and so on. Making the mealtime sacred will take an intentional effort on your part. Not every paragraph or sentence has to have the name of God invoked somewhere, but focusing the meal around spirituality won't happen spontaneously, at least not at first. A variety of ways offer themselves to center the mealtime conversation on the spiritual realm. You'll probably need to try several before you find the ones that work for your family.

- Ask spiritually leading questions such as, "Where did you see God in your day?" and, "How was God working in your lives today?"
- Ask general spiritual and religious questions to spark a discussion (and make sure the children get to answer fully): "How do you picture the face of God? What do you think the afterlife (or heaven) is like?" or, "Why do you think God allowed so many religions in the world?[9]"
- Read a Bible passage aloud and discuss it using the Discovery Questions.[10]

- Lead a devotional using a family devotional book.
- Pause the mealtime for a brief prayer whenever someone mentions a need (such as a sick friend, an upcoming test they're anxious about, and so on).
- Choose a news story and talk about its spiritual implications. (How is God working here? Why did this happen? What could Hitchhikers do about it? What should you as a family do about it?)

When the meal is over, mark the end of the spiritual time. You can do this with a closing prayer, by singing a song (that's how some sacred meals in the Bible are ended), or by taking turns pronouncing a blessing upon the family.

> As we leave the table
> Filled with good food and good thoughts
> May we see God in each of us
> As we go our way this evening.

Family Prayer

Prayer is, unfortunately, a touchy subject even in the family. When the children are young, they are fearless in their prayers. As they grow older, children develop a tendency to become self-conscious. I think we become almost paranoid that our prayers won't be PC (Poetically Correct). We're convinced they don't sound as good as other people's prayers. Let me share a little secret with you: Even most of us clergy with multiple degrees behind our names think our out-loud praying is inadequate. The exceptions tend to be when someone writes prayers in advance and then memorizes them or reads them aloud. On the other hand, if you make a regular habit of praying together as a family from the time the children are young, with a bit of encouragement and blessings from the Spirit, your children may never experience these fears.

In any event, prayer is the most important spiritual habit you and your family can develop. For one, prayer is the only tool we've been given that will reach the spiritual realm from our world. Even the apostles knew prayer was the most important habit of all. We have no record of the twelve asking Jesus to teach them how to heal people, how to cast out demons, or how to feed thousands with a couple of loaves and fishes. Instead, they asked Jesus to teach them just one thing: "Lord, teach us to pray" (Luke 11:1). Notice, they didn't ask for instruction on how to pray. They asked Jesus to teach them *to* pray—to teach them to *do* it. Prayer remains the spiritual practice most needed in our world today.

Perhaps our fears should be less about *how* we pray than the fact that we *don't do it* enough.

Making prayer a priority in your family's lives first depends on your attitude toward prayer. If prayer is just an afterthought or if you only turn to prayer in times when a Hail Mary pass to the end zone is called for, then you probably won't raise a praying family. On the other hand, if you sprinkle your prayers throughout your normal, everyday life, then your family will likely follow suit if you encourage them.

You have a choice of ways to introduce prayer to your family (bedtime prayers, table grace, etc.), I want to share two that I consider the most important and effective practices. If you add these two practices into your family's repertoire of spiritual habits, Hitchhiker's Evangelism with your children almost takes care of itself.

Just-in-Time Prayer

I remember many occasions when someone has asked me to pray for them. I'd agree with good intentions, only to remember to pray sometime later—sometimes *much* later. Who knows how many other times I've heard people express some sort of a need that I allowed to go unnoticed and unprayed for. After hearing a song on the radio about good intentions but lack of practicing prayer for others, I began a personal campaign to pray in the then and now. Just-in-Time Prayer takes seriously the power of prayer in our lives by making prayer a priority.

Practicing Just-in-Time Prayer is simply a matter of listening with a prayerful ear. Whenever someone expresses a need, stop whatever you're doing—even to the point of interrupting the conversation—and offer to pray with them. Notice the key word, you're offering to pray *with* them as opposed to praying *for* them. For instance, let's say that during breakfast your spouse mentions they're going to be facing a tough client later in the day. Instead of saying, "Good luck" or "I'll pray for you," take their hand and say, "Let me pray with you." Then offer a quick, but heartfelt, prayer.[11] If your children are in the room, have them come and put their hand on yours as you pray. You could even ask them to pray (especially after you've modeled this kind of praying a couple of times).

Offer this kind of prayer whenever an opportunity arises. If your little one gets an boo-boo or your teenager tells you about an upcoming test, pray with them then and there. The key to learning the importance of prayer is modeling its importance. Pray with them before they go to school, work, or on a date. Pray with them when they don't feel well, when they're worried about their grades, or they are experiencing a troubled relationship. Don't forget to pray with them whenever they mention a concern for the neighbor's health, a friend's misfortune, or a news event they're concerned about. As you model Just-in-Time Prayer and as it becomes commonplace in your home, encourage the rest of the family to put it into practice as well.

One last word about Just-in-Time Prayer! If you've created sacred time during your meals, one of the conversations you can regularly initiate is to ask about prayers that were offered earlier in the day. For instance, asking your spouse how it went with the tough client you prayed for is a great way to help the family see the connection between the spiritual realm and the here and now. Indeed, I've found these kinds of conversations eventually stimulate a reliance on prayer, because the family becomes aware that God's hand really is a part of their lives.

Set-Aside Prayer

Whereas spontaneous Just-in-Time Prayer invites the family to see God's hand intervening in their lives, Set-Aside Prayer balances prayer in regards to our needs as opposed to prayer as time spent with God. Although God's omnipresence means God is always with us no matter what or where, most of the time we're blissfully unaware of that reality. Although the Divine invites us to pray for our needs and desires, these are not meant to be the only objects of our prayer. God is not a super Santa in the sky whose primary role is to grant us unending wishes. Immanuel means "God with us" and suggests we're to reciprocate and "be with God."

I've known a lot of Hitchhikers over the years who have tried and failed repeatedly to develop family devotions. I've also been on the receiving end of pastors berating their congregations about it and have left these services feeling more guilty than inspired to do better.

Set-Aside Prayer is a little like family devotions in that you need to be intentional about creating regular sacred time to practice it. On the other hand, it's unlike family devotions in other rather important ways. For one, although it would be ideal to practice Set-Aside Prayer with your family every day, I'm suggesting that you create this time but once a week. For another, the purpose of Set-Aside Prayer is to pray. Nothing else. No Bible readings, no devotional commentaries, and no discussions. Just prayer. Now, this might sound a bit intimidating or even unworkable in your family setting, but let me assure you, even if you have three-year-old triplets, you can add this important prayer time.

The primary purpose of Set-Aside Prayer is to spend time in conversation with the Divine. Whereas in Just-in-Time Prayer you go to

God with specific requests, in Set-Aside Prayer you will spend time in worship, gratitude, listening, a bit of groveling, and in asking for some direction.

Practicing Set-Aside Prayer has a secondary purpose. Many Christians confess that they don't really know how to pray effectively. By practicing Set-Aside Prayer just once a week, in a short time you and your family will not only know how to pray, you'll become more comfortable praying.

Set-Aside Prayer is based on Jesus' response to the apostles' question about praying and uses one of the best known prayers of all times: the Lord's Prayer. However, instead of just reciting it, as many of us were taught to do when we went to worship services, you'll use the prayer as an outline for your family's prayers.

Before launching into how to pray, though, let's talk about when to pray. Like I said earlier, I suggest you set aside one day a week for this prayer time. The day and time you set is up to you, but I suggest adding this prayer time to the end of your Sunday lunch or dinner. Historically, the Friday evening meal is another excellent time to add this prayer because it marks the beginning of the Sabbath day. Your family could gather before or after church on Sunday morning for prayer or at any time that is convenient and conducive for praying together. You may want to disconnect this from normal Sunday worship times and set aside one evening time during the week to gather the whole family for your family's special prayer time.

Regardless of when you set aside time for praying, you will want to ensure you won't be interrupted or rushed. If you have young children or if you're just adding this time to your family's agenda, plan on spending ten to fifteen minutes in prayer. However, as you grow accustomed to Set-Aside Prayer, you may find even thirty minutes to be insufficient time, so ask family members to make this a priority appointment and to refrain from planning appointments that might steal from the appointment with God. Then turn off the television, the telephone, the cell phones, the computers that may announce e-mail, the stereos, and anything else that might interrupt your time so that you can begin to pray.

Praying the Set-Aside Prayer is a matter of learning to use the Lord's Prayer as an outline rather than to pray it by rote. The prayer has six natural divisions, or parts. Each one invites you and your family to build on the division's theme. For instance, you begin the time by praying the first theme, which is praise and worship: "Our Father, which art in heaven. Hallowed be thy name" (Mt. 6:9, KJV).[12] Then, for the next few minutes, you and your family offer prayers that echo the theme. Young children might offer prayers that recognize what God is doing in the world: "God, thank you for the sunshine you made," or "I liked the rainbow you put in the sky on Monday." Teenagers might be encouraged to consider some of the names and attributes of God mentioned throughout the Bible: "Lord, you kept me safe this week at football practice—you have been my shield." Adults might offer words that emphasize the holiness or awesomeness of God: "God, you are the ruler of the universe and yet you care for us. Thank you."

Remember to keep the prayer time informal, especially with young children and with those who don't have significant previous church experience. Eyes don't necessarily need to be closed, and conversation doesn't need to be limited to monologues about God; indeed, it should be directed *to* God. A Set-Aside Prayer time for the first theme could look something like this:

Parent: Our Father, which art in heaven. Hallowed be thy name. Cindy, what are you thankful to God for?

Three-Year-Old Cindy: Thank you for the pretty flowers and the clouds.

Parent: God, I'm amazed at the beauty of your creation, but even more amazed that you have watched over us so well this week. Chris, are there any names or attributes of God that you've seen this week?

Fifteen-Year-Old Chris: Yeah. Your Spirit has helped me keep my attitude under control—thanks for that.

Parent: Thy kingdom come, thy will be done, in earth as it is in heaven.

You will discover that as the family gets used to praying together, the need for prompting even the youngest of children will diminish significantly.

Now, let's look at the Lord's Prayer as an outline for Set-Aside Prayer:

Our Father, which art in heaven, hallowed be thy name. Offer prayers of praise, worship, thanksgiving, and recognizing the names and attributes of God.

Thy kingdom come, thy will be done, in earth as it is in heaven. Pray that your leaders will do God's will (parents; pastors; employers; teachers; local, national, and international leaders). Also pray here about any decisions being considered by members of the family.

Give us this day our daily bread. Pray for needs and desires.

Forgive us our debts as we forgive our debtors. This division is pretty self-evident, but make sure to address anyone family members may be having difficulty forgiving.

Lead us not into temptation, but deliver us from evil. This is a good time to recognize those things that are temptations to the various family members. Name them, and pray about them. Also take notice of the second part of this section: asking the Spirit to keep family members away from places of temptation—a good prayer for children and adults alike.

For thine is the kingdom, and the power, and the glory forever. The last part of the prayer nearly mimics the first part, except this time the focus is on acknowledging that everything belongs to God and that God is in charge. Pray for those things family members may need to let go of, such as selfishness or independence, and at the other end of the continuum, self-deprecation or low self-esteem.

Creating a faith-filled atmosphere at home is one of the most effective ways to bring your family to faith. Couple that with personal integrity and the humility to take personal responsibility even in front of your children, and you can be sure the witness you present will provide the best opportunity to usher your family into the kingdom of God.

By the Way Reflections

1. When you've had a hard day, how do you express your emotions at home? What kind of an impact do you think this has had on your family?
2. What about being at home makes it easier or more difficult to effectively reflect your faith?
3. Ultimately, do you think it's the parent's job or the church's job to pass on the Christian faith to their children? Why?
4. According to Carla Williams, a specialist in children's spiritual development, churched parents often feel unprepared to teach their children how to practice the basics of the faith (prayer, meditation, fasting, devotions, and so on).[13] Why do you think this is?
5. What sort of emotions do you experience when you think about the words accountability and confession?
6. Whom do you know who would benefit from being in a Journey Group Partnership? What would keep you from starting one with that person?
7. What could you do to make your home more of a spiritual refuge?

NOTES

[1]Egon Mayer, Barry A. Kosmin, and Ariela Keysar, *American Religious Identification Survey* (New York: Graduate Center of the City of New York University, 2001), http://www.gc.cuny.edu/faculty/research_briefs/aris/key_findings.htm.

[2]"Surveys Show Pastors Claim Congregants Are Deeply Committed to God But Congregants Deny It!" *The Barna Update,* January 9, 2006, http://www.barna.org/FlexPage.aspx?Page=BarnaUpdateNarrow&BarnaUpdateID=206.

[3]The Jewish Christians who met in the synagogues did have access to the Hebrew Scriptures, but non-Jewish believers did not. And though Paul's letters and eventually the gospels were widely circulated, they would not have been universally available. Acts 17:1–10, which tells of the founding of the church in Thessalonica, shows Paul was able to plant a church that became "a model to all the believers in Macedonia and Achaia" (1 Thess. 1:7) in only three weeks—without a Bible.

[4]*The Apostolic Traditions of Hippolytus of Rome,* trans. Kevin P. Edgecomb (2000), http://www.bombaxo.com/hippolytus.html.

[5]See *House Church Manual* (St. Louis: Chalice Press, 2004) and *High-Voltage Spirituality* (St. Louis: Chalice Press, 2006).

[6]What is or what is not reasonable has limits. If you missed your seven-year-old's soccer game that you said you'd attend, the child's demands that you quit your job so it never happens again is probably unreasonable. On the other hand, if that's the demand, you probably need to examine your priorities because this probably wasn't the first time you broke your promise. Make an inviolable plan to do better—and make it *inviolable.*

[7]See www.christiansymbols.net for a compendium of other symbols.

[8]For a discussion of decorating for sacred space, see *High Voltage Spirituality.*

[9]Gary Poole's *The Complete Book of Questions* (Grand Rapids: Zondervan, 2003) offers over a thousand questions useful for conversations, many of which are spiritual in nature.

[10]See appendix C.

[11]I use this same practice with friends and even brand new acquaintances, with one modification. I always ask, "May I pray for you about that?" I've *never* had anyone turn me down—even in public. In fact, most express shock and awe and ask something like, "You'd do that for me?" I nod, put my hand on their shoulder, and pray a brief prayer. When I finish, I assure them I'll continue to pray. It's amazing the on-the-way evangelism opportunities this opens as time goes by and the relationship grows.

[12]I've presented the prayer in the *King James Version* because it's the version most commonly memorized and the most familiar to most people.

[13]Carla Williams, *As You Walk Along the Way* (Camp Hill, Pa.: Horizon Books, 2001), 30.

CHAPTER SEVEN

Getting Radical

Let's Give Them Something to Talk About

If anyone comes to me and does not hate father and mother, wife and children, brothers and sisters—yes, even life itself—such a person cannot be my disciple. (Lk. 14:26)

Jesus occasionally made some outrageous statements:

Leave everything.

Embrace persecution.

Eat my flesh and drink my blood.

It's easier to get a camel through a needle than for the wealthy to enter the kingdom of God.

Hate your mom and dad.

Most Christians would rather water down, dismiss, or ignore completely these hard sayings. But once in a while, people come along and assume Jesus meant what he said. They embrace a radical lifestyle. Strange people, or so we think.

So far, most of what you've read in this book is pretty tame. Oh sure, here and there you've heard the call to step out of your comfort zone, but all in all what you've read could hardly be considered revolutionary. Evangelism with your friends, where you shop, while you're at work, when you're at the club, or with your family. Tame. Mild. Anything *but* radical.

On the other hand, this short chapter is about radical evangelism. It's about practices that demand a second look and even deserve a dinnertime conversation. Radical evangelism is a commitment to sharing the Gospel that goes beyond the ordinary. It's about making the faith not just a priority, but *the* priority in your life, above and beyond anything else. Period. Some of what you read may inspire you. I'll be honest, some may appall you. These accounts aren't just untried radical fantasies. Hitchhikers with courage, commitment, and clarity across North America have embraced these evangelistic lifestyles that demand to be shared, considered, and perhaps even emulated by some brave and hearty souls who are committed above all else to the Gospel.

Defining Radical

No matter how far over the top someone is, one person's radical is someone else's ho-hum. So, where do I draw the line? That part is easy. If the evangelism practice is outside of the mainstream if it would generate comments, supportive or not, and if it cost more than the average, everyday Christian was willing to pay, then it was at least considered. The list includes practices that could change your dress code, change your address, and change either your vocation or your avocation.

Change the Way You Look

Generally speaking, you can't tell the difference between a Hitchhiker, a Nomad, or a Wanderer by the way they look. Sure, the dress code of some Christians like Blaine in chapter 4 includes branded T-shirts that are matched only by Blaine's personal zeal for in-your-face prophetic confrontation. Honestly, even with all the Blaines in the world, the vast majority of us Hitchhikers are pretty nondescript.

Long ago the only way you could tell someone was a Christian by his or her dress was if they were wearing some sort of a habit. Only the "professional religious" were the bearers of the "religious look." From the clerical collar to the tonsure haircut, from the nun's coronet to the monastic alb, the garb of religion was reserved for those who were in the full-time employ of the church.

Today, the religious look has taken on some new dimensions. Although much of the religious garb continues to be exclusive to clergy and monastics, some have redefined the terms while others have found new ways to express their faith by changing how they look. Let's look at two trends in radically changing the way you look as an expression of faith and as a tool for sharing the faith.

Tatting

The ancient art of tatting, fine needlework that creates patterns and art that lasts a generation, is making a profound comeback. No, I'm not talking about lace making, I'm talking about body art and, more specifically, tattooing.

In Leviticus 19:28, the Mosaic law prohibits the Israelites from getting tattoos. The prohibition is snuggled in amongst commands against trimming your beard or sideburns, wearing cotton-blend shirts, mules, and any pay period longer than a day. Today, with the rising popularity of body art, a hue and cry against the practice has been heralded across the land. The Internet hosts literally hundreds of articles against Christian tattooing, each one citing the Leviticus passage as part of their rationale. A growing Christian industry specializes in removing these "marks of the beast."

I'm not going to devote a lot of space to defending the practice of using Christian tattoos as a radical evangelism tool, except to make this observation. It's awfully funny how some Christians pick and choose which of the Levitical laws still apply. We'll happily break the Levitical laws by wearing cotton-polyester blends, keeping our sideburns trimmed, shaving our facial hair, eating shrimp or lobster, paying our employees by the week or the month, and frankly, I don't believe I've ever heard a sermon against mules.[1] On the other hand, I have heard sermons against guys with long hair, women wearing jeans or makeup, and lately against body piercing and tattoos.

In recent years, the popularity of body art has boomed in North America. Its popularity isn't just among teens and twenty-somethings either. Even professionals and seniors are getting tattooed, though they tend to be more conservative about where they have their body art placed. Indeed, once reserved for bikers and sailors, tattooing has become almost mainstream.

Evangelizing with Ink

A number of Hitchhikers have embraced the practice. They use their tats as conversation starters and faith-sharing opportunities. I came across this post made by a passing visitor on an Internet blog:

> I have a very well done Chi Rho tattoo that serves several functions:
> (1) it draws my mind to Christ throughout the day when I see it
> (2) is a great tool for evangelism, as I am constantly asked what it is, which has generated many very interesting conversations, and (3) it looks really cool.[2]

This post only scratches the surface of inked Christians. The Christian Tattoo Association, founded by Daniel Ostrowski, Rand Johnson, and Randy Mastre, is a growing organization of tattoo artists, clients, and aficionados. The association was initially formed to reach tattoo artists with the Gospel, but over the years it has also been instrumental in providing information and advice to many would-be tattooed evangelists. According to Ostrowski, "The tattoo world has been a dark world for so long. We needed to bring light in a dark place."[3]

Joe Scinta has been a Christian for years, but he got inked for Jesus after he turned forty. His tattoo depicts Jesus carrying him when he could no longer carry himself (see illustration). He got the tattoo specifically as a testimony to his faith, and it's been a door opener for many opportunities.

> The first person I got to share my faith with was the guy doing the tattoo. He wanted to know what it was all about, so I was able to share my faith story. I've gone to a couple of bike rallies and had several guys ask about it. Some of them don't know anything about Jesus, so it's cool because I can tell them about him. One biker asked me about the tattoo, and I was able to share the Gospel. He didn't ask many questions, but he was interested. I don't know what he'll do with it, but I planted some seeds. The tattoo has opened up doors that wouldn't be there otherwise.[4]

Ramifications of Being Tatted

If you're not already tatted, before you rush off to get eternally inked, take some time to reflect on what you're about to embark upon. To begin with, you'll want to consider the ramifications of getting a tattoo in the first place, especially a faith-based tattoo. Remember this is just one element of radical evangelism and is not for everyone. The following list comes from conversations I've had with a number of tatted Christians.

- Some Christians will be judgmental about your tat. Be ready for the occasional onslaught of how evil you are (remember, a number of the religious folk said the same thing about Jesus).
- Tats are permanent. Yes, they can come off with a rather expensive laser procedure, but the process leaves some scarring.

- Some employers will not hire people who have visible tattoos, so unless you have a stable, permanent job and they're accepting about tats, be careful what part of your body you use as canvas.
- Some employers have strict policies about expressions of religious beliefs that could be applied to a faith-based tat.
- When you get a tattoo, you will not be able to donate blood to the Red Cross for twelve months, unless your state is one of the few that strictly regulates the sterility of tattoo parlors.
- Your skin is quite elastic, but like a rubber band, once it stretches, it never quite returns to its original size. If you're overweight and get a tattoo, the tattoo may not retain its original proportions when you lose significant weight,.
- Aging causes your skin to lose some of its elasticity as well. If you get a tattoo when you're young, as you age the tattoo may lose its original proportions.

The Process

If you've thought through the ramifications and you're still committed to getting inked for Jesus, you need to do some homework before you head down to visit your local tattoo studio. You need to make some very important decisions before you put your body into the hands of an ink artist.

Choosing the canvas. The first decision is deciding where are you're going to put the tattoo. If you're honestly getting a tat for evangelism, it will need to be where others can see it without their being embarrassed to look at it. Conversely, if you put a tat where you can't cover it, you might have employment difficulties. According to Marisa Kakoulas, a tatted New York lawyer, most companies can legally refuse to hire you if you wear a tattoo that can't be covered. Indeed, if you work in the private sector, an employer can almost certainly fire you if you even get a tattoo. You would probably have no legal recourse.[5] Many people, therefore, opt to put tats on their upper arms, ankles, or lower legs. All three of these body parts are easily covered by standard articles of clothing. However, these provide fairly limited canvases for artwork, which takes us to the next bit of homework you'll need to do.

Choosing the design. Although you could tour all the local tattoo studios in hopes of finding an inspiring work of flash[6] on their walls, your best bet is to thoughtfully and prayerfully decide in advance exactly what you want permanently inked on your body. You can get far too easily excited about cool flash and impulsively decide *that's* the image for your arm. Tattoos are (or should be) extremely personal. In the end, the design you choose will be with you for the rest of your life, so don't let yourself get caught up in the moment. The design choice will need to stand the test of time. You should also keep in mind that the point of this exercise is to elicit faith-sharing opportunities. Take enough time to seriously contemplate what sort of an image intersects with your spirit and would raise the curiosity of others.

You need to realize that the canvas you choose will limit the scope of your design choice. If you want a detailed image of the Last Supper, it wouldn't fit very well on your upper arm—even sideways! On the

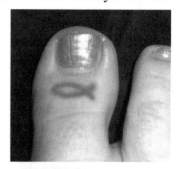

other hand, if you want the symbol (the Christian fish image), you could put it on a space as small as your big toe. My wife has a red chalice tat on her ankle, the symbol of communion as well as her denomination's logo. Our son, on the other hand, designed a Celtic cross that includes his two adoption dates: the date of his earthly adoption into my family lineage, and the date of his baptism, his adoption into the family of God. His design was too big to effectively fit on his shoulder, so he had it inked onto his back. It's generally only visible to the world when he's at the beach.

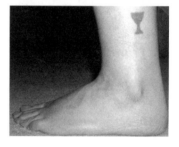

The design choices you can make for your eternal ink are virtually limitless. If you need inspiration, Google *tattoo* and *flash* and *Christian* for thousands of Web sites with examples.

Once you've chosen a design, print a quality hard copy approximately the same size as you want the image on your body. Then, and only then, can you start looking for a quality artist.

Find a tattoo artist. Once upon a time, finding a tattoo studio meant going to the seediest part of town and trusting your safety and your health to luck. Things have changed significantly over the past few years. In most larger communities today you'll discover you have several, if not many, studios and artists to choose from. Since tattooing is more mainstream than ever before, you do not need to trust to luck to find a quality artist or shop.

You can find a talented artist in several ways, but probably the safest way is to depend on referrals. In general, most people with tattoos love to talk about them, so if you see a passing stranger with some great ink, and you're the outgoing type, you can feel free to ask where they got it and who their artist was. However, most neophytes find it less intimidating to ask for recommendations from their tattooed friends. If they've had a good experience, they'll probably recommend their artist. If they had a not-so-good experience, they'll warn you off.

When our middle daughter celebrated her eighteenth birthday, she decided to get her first tattoo so she began asking her friends and folks she met who were tattooed about local tattoo artists. Several of her friends highly recommended a particular artist and a particular studio, so she enlisted my wife to accompany her on a reconnaissance mission. My daughter has acquired eight tattoos and is the family expert. In preparing to write this section, I called and asked her opinion about finding a quality studio. She gave me plenty of advice, but I found her comment about cleanliness to be the most instructive. "When I check out a studio, I first depend on the smell to help me decide. If the studio doesn't smell like a clean hospital when I walk in, I walk out."[7]

Two primary considerations come into play when it comes to choosing a studio and an artist. First, as my daughter pointed out, make sure it's a clean studio. Although the CDC says that no known cases of AIDS have been contracted through tattooing, once upon a time Hepatitis B was commonly spread between customers at tattoo parlors. Tattoo salons have largely cleaned up their act since the dark days of reusable needles and autoclaves. Indeed, state health departments monitor tattoo studios for cleanliness and sterility. Reputable shops utilize single-use tattoo needles for their clients. This ensures that the needles have come from a sterile environment. Couple that with careful cleanliness of the work areas and health risks drop to very low levels.

Assuming the studio is clean, the second consideration is the quality of the art. Tattoo artists are *artists* and enjoy displaying their work. Besides getting recommendations from others, you need to examine an artist's portfolio with photographs of their work. Again, don't get in a hurry to go under the needle. Ask to see the artist's work, and scrutinize it carefully. Remember, this is a lifetime investment—you want it to be right.

Getting inked. When you've done all your homework, and you've thought and prayed really hard about getting tattooed for Jesus, it's time to take the plunge. Today, some studios demand clients make appointments, but many still operate on a first-in, first-served basis. Since you've been to the studio and spoken to the artist at least once, you already know their procedures. Either make an appointment, go early, or go later. Enjoy the conversation at the parlor while you wait. It's best to take a trusted friend with you for moral support and to drive you home lest you feel woozy. Tattooing can be a rather painful process, though many folk get used to it (our daughter slept through one of her tattoo applications). Once you've been inked, listen carefully to the after-care procedures and follow them to the letter. Some great tattoos have gone bad because the clients disregarded the care instructions. Remember, this is a lifetime investment—make sure you do it right.

Once you're tatted up, the rest is pretty much up to you and the Holy Spirit. When someone notices your tat and asks a question about it, consider it a Divine appointment. Take the opportunity to share your faith story. This isn't the time to be pushy, but it's not the time to be timid either. I close this section with a quote from Daniel Ostrowski:

> Some Christians meet new people, and they are afraid the people they're meeting will find out they're born again; I'm afraid I'll meet someone and they won't know I'm born again. I want everybody I meet to know I'm nuts for Jesus.[8]

Habits

When most of us hear the word *habit*, images of nail biting, smoking, or fiddling with our tresses flit through our minds. However, some of the habits radical Hitchhikers are picking up have nothing to do with bad behaviors, but alternative clothing.

More and more committed Hitchhikers are dropping out of the rat race to embrace the monastic way of life. I'll introduce these neomonastics later in this chapter, but some of these cultural dropouts aren't just trading in their Beemers and corporate identities for a spiritual way of life. They're actually trading their jeans for the monastic habit. Monastic garb has been a distinction of religious orders for well over a thousand years. A monk's habit includes the tunic, scapular, and hood. Nuns wear the tunic and scapular, but rather than a hood, they wear a wimple and veil.

Though the Roman and Orthodox Catholic churches have been the primary sponsors of monastic movements, some Protestant denominations are hosts to monastic religious orders as well. These organized bodies aren't the only ones with monastic communities, nor are they the only ones who get into a habit.

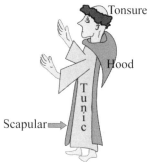

Today a growing number of neomonastic communities around the world, as well as in North America, embrace the practice of wearing the habit. Although few of the communities approve wearing the monastic garb beyond the bounds of the communal setting, some of these settings are fairly fluid. For instance, the Lindisfarne Community based in Ithaca, New York, and the Knights of Prayer Monastic Order based in Portland, Oregon, extend their monastic umbrella to monks-in-the-world wherever they may be. The Lindisfarne Community's habit is a white cassock or alb with a three-knot black rope cincture tied around the waist. Members may wear the habit whenever they practice prayer, meditation, or the liturgies of the community. The Knights of Prayer monastics wear a forest green hooded tunic and a dark emerald green scapular. Full members in residence may wear the habit daily, while members living outside of the community may wear the habit only when in prayer. Of course, new monastic communities, both physical and community based, are popping up all over the world, so you may start seeing habits in the street sometime soon.

Change How You Live

What's life like in your community?

Careful—that's a loaded question. Your response ought to be, *Which community?* Is the query about your city, suburb, town, or countryside? Perhaps it's about your church—your faith community. If you're a student, the question could be about your learning community. If you're employed, the inquiry might be about your work community. The conversation may go in many directions when you start talking about community.

Living *in community,* however, is rather different than living in *a* community. If you live with your family, you are living "in community" with your household members. The new movement called neomonasticism (new-monasticism, nu-monasticism) hearkens back to the early church in Acts and the way they modeled community.

The Apostle's Model

The evening before the day of Pentecost about 33 A.D., the Christian Way included 120 Hitchhikers. Twenty-four hours later, they had 3,000 brand new believers. Now, let's be honest for a moment. Most churches would be left reeling if they had an influx of even 100 new members in a single day, but 3,000 new members? Where do you seat 3,000 new church members when you don't even have a building? How do you disciple brand new believers without so much as a Bible, let alone a curriculum? But apparently, someone had a plan. Instead of starting a building campaign or hiring thirty full-time staff members, the early church leaders created community.

We all have an idea about what community is, sort of. The definitions include such insights as people interacting in a common location, sharing common characteristics, common interests, or living together within a larger society. The community the apostles created had all of these aspects to some degree, but ultimately it was so much more.

Let's take a quick look at some of the first faith community's characteristics by reviewing what the book of Acts says about how they lived and worked together:

- They were committed to spending time in both study and fellowship with their mentors (2:42).
- They prayed and seemed to have shared Communion together (2:42).
- They spent significant daily time together (2:44).
- They held their possessions in community (2:44; 4:32).
- They contributed their wages and sold their possessions to help support those of the community who were in need (2:45; 4:34).
- They sold excess properties as needed for the community (4:34).
- They came together daily as a larger community (2:46).
- They got together for shared meals in their homes (2:46).
- They worshiped in their homes (2:47).

On the other hand, look at what the passages *didn't* say:

- They didn't live in the same house, neighborhood, or monastery.
- Even though they held their possessions and wages in community, they didn't live in the streets. They continued to reside in their own houses.
- They didn't worship as an organized single body in the temple.[9]

The community described in the book of Acts lived the ideals of the camp song "They'll know we are Christians by our love." The result of their community life was clearly evangelistic: "They enjoyed the favor of the public and the Lord added to the church daily those who were being saved" (2:47, paraphrased). Indeed, the church took such good care of each other that by the end of the second century it had to adopt a training and trial period of up to three years (catechism), in part to keep freeloaders from hindering the church's ability to care for itself. Bear in mind that the church was the people, not buildings or staff, and the shared funds primarily went to care for the working poor and those who could not work.[10]

The Monastic Model

In 312 A.D. Constantine promoted Christianity as the new state religion after defeating Maxentius at the Milvian Bridge near Rome. In 313, at the behest of his mother Helena, he built the first dedicated church building. From that first building in Bethlehem, Constantine's church building program took wings. Soon churches were popping up all across the empire. The building program was accompanied with a change in how the church organized and oversaw itself. It was all too much for some Hitchhikers who seemed to have concluded that the church had lost its spiritual foundations, so they withdrew from "civilization" to return to the presence of God. Many found refuge and solace in the Egyptian desert, while others preferred the wilds of Palestine, Syria, and Arabia. Solitude was the watchword for many of these first wilderness dwellers, but in time many became well known for their spiritual wisdom. As their renown grew, so did the pilgrims who left the comforts of civilization to sit at the feet of these desert Abbas and Ammas.[11] Eventually those who embraced the ways of simplicity and prayer built monasteries, developed rules, and created community.

The monastic model has similarities to the apostle's model, but with significant differences. Monastic living is shared living in every sense of the word:

- The community resides together in group housing, though each typically has their own cell, or bedroom.
- Community members tend to take a vow of poverty, share a common purse, and lay claim to no possessions.
- The community shares their day together, typically using a *horarium* or "liturgy of the hours" that governs the schedule of community rising, prayer, meals, work, rest, and repose.
- The community lives under a common "rule" as their guide for communal living.

Eventually, the scope of monastic living changed from simply sharing quarters; instead, the community was defined by its obedience to an abbot or abbess. This freed monastics to move and/or live around the countryside as their superior allowed and is the basis on which much of the neomonastic movement is built.

Neomonasticism

Whether you call it neo, new, or nu-monasticism, a spiritually aesthetic movement is brewing in the West. These monastic communities are forming in much the same way as the first desert mothers and fathers began them in Egypt. You may have noticed a mass exodus from the established church in the United States and Canada—to the tune of over a million church members a year for the past several years.[12] People give many reasons for dropping out of the church: irrelevance, hypocrisy, cliquishness, and church infighting to name but a few. None of these reasons explain the rise of neo-monasticism.

At a time when the church had grown too cozy with the ruling authorities, when faith had become a means to power and influence, some Christians who sought to live out an authentically biblical faith headed for desolate places. They pooled their resources and dedicated themselves to a life of asceticism and prayer. Most outsiders thought they were crazy. They saw themselves as being on the narrow and difficult path of salvation, with a call to prick the conscience of the wider church about its compromises with the "world."[13] These words sound like the monastics of the fourth century, but Jason Byassee is describing the current state of affairs in where some hearty souls are leaving culture's comforts to embrace poverty, insignificance, chastity, and obedience in community.

No one really knows how many of these new monastic-styled communities are popping up across the nation, but they seem to be forming in nearly every major city. In the fall of 2003, Jonathan Wilson-Hartgrove, a Duke University student, proposed a project to invite between ten and twenty folks who were involved in monastic-like communities to come together and discuss what was emerging as a new monasticism. Much to Jonathan's chagrin, in June of 2004 over sixty people from across the nation showed up for the conference. From Roman Catholics to Anabaptists, Mainliners to Evangelicals, interest in the topic drew practitioners and scholars alike. Although each community was markedly different in style and rule, common themes and practices emerged as the participants shared their stories and their learnings. By the end of the conference, the participants had created a document they felt captured the heart of this budding movement. They called the report the "Twelve Marks of a New Monasticism":

1. Relocation to the abandoned places of Empire.
2. Sharing economic resources with fellow community members and the needy among us.
3. Hospitality to the stranger.
4. Lament for racial divisions within the church and our communities combined with the active pursuit of a just reconciliation.
5. Humble submission to Christ's body, the church.
6. Intentional formation in the way of Christ and the rule of the community along the lines of the old novitiate.
7. Nurturing common life among members of intentional community.
8. Support for celibate singles alongside monogamous married couples and their children.
9. Geographical proximity to community members who share a common rule of life.
10. Care for the plot of God's earth given to us along with support of our local economies.
11. Peacemaking in the midst of violence and conflict resolution within communities along the lines of Matthew 18.
12. Commitment to a disciplined contemplative life.[14]

As you can see from the list, in the eyes of most churchgoers, it would take a pretty radical Hitchhiker to leave their comfy suburb to relocate to the "abandoned places of the Empire." This implies that the neo-monastics are mostly heading for the urban centers across the nation, though some have found rural spaces that, for all practical purposes, seem abandoned by the empire. The neo-monasteries can be found in places like Camden, New Jersey, widely known as one of the most polluted cities in the United States as well as the Kensington neighborhood in Philadelphia, known for its bombed-out look of 700 abandoned factories. These are some of the poorest neighborhoods in the United States and are rife with crime, violence, drug addicts, poverty, and a pervasive hopelessness. You probably wouldn't be surprised to spy Dante's warning at these neighborhoods' borders: "*Lasciate ogni speranza ch'entrate.*" (Abandon hope all who enter here.) Even so, the neo-monastics are traveling to these urban wastelands to buy dilapidated buildings and turn them into homes. More than homes, these are outposts of Jesus' love. The neo-monasteries are ministries of presence.

It takes a serious commitment to Jesus and the church of the New Testament to live in a neo-monastic community. This is no place for ideologues, hence the sixth mark calling for a commitment to the novitiate. Most of the existing communities entertain visitors and welcome interns, many of whom come from nearby seminaries. Those who want to join are generally treated to at least a year of training and examination by the whole community before they are fully embraced. Living in a community that eschews society's upward mobility emphasis can be difficult, especially for families. Dr. Jenell Williams Paris, associate professor of anthropology at Bethel University, lived in a neo-monastic setting for eight years before moving on. "[American] culture is set up for married people with careers and kids to live in houses and to be mobile as a unit."[15] Living among the poorest people in the city and sending your children to the nearest public school isn't for the feeble at heart.

Still, relocating and living with the poor and the outcasts wherever they may congregate is exactly the tactic used by Saint Francis and Mother Teresa, heroes of the Christian faith. Indeed, Ray Bakke, an urban theologian, insists that it's time for the suburban churches to begin "tithing" their members to these very places. He cites Nehemiah 11:1–2 as the source of his inspiration:

> Now the leaders of the people settled in Jerusalem. The rest of the people cast lots to bring one out of every ten of them to live in Jerusalem, the holy city, while the remaining nine were to stay in their own towns. The people commended all who volunteered to live in Jerusalem. (TNIV)

Not much has changed since Nehemiah's day. Even then, nobody wanted to live in the big bad city, so the faithful drew lots and sent 10 percent to relocate to the city where, for several generations, the poor and the ignorant had struggled to eke out an existence. Bakke asserts that the most effective urban evangelization efforts begin by relocating committed disciples to work and live in these urban mission fields (like Camden, Philadelphia, Los Angeles, Seattle, and others).[16] Outside do-gooders who come to do "ministry" are automatically suspect by the residents of these neighborhoods. Experience has taught these "recipients of grace" that the attitude of the "haves" is that the "have-nots" are second-class citizens in need of being patronizingly cared for. They've learned they are worthy enough to receive pity, but not worthy enough to be neighbors. They've found that do-gooders come and go, but the problems downtown remain unchanged. A bandage from the outside will not cure an infection; it takes an antibiotic that works from the inside out. The neo-monastic communities are intentional about becoming neighbors who invest in the community from the inside by investing in their neighbors. They don't just talk the talk, they are Hitchhikers who have shed their pretenses to be Jesus in the heart of their cities.

So, what's it like to live in community as a radical Hitchhiker? Every neo-monastery is different. Some share a single house; others share a neighborhood. A few follow a liturgy of the hours complete with scheduled prayer times; others do not. Some share a common purse; others require a set percentage. At least one community receives all the funds but returns a set amount per family for living expenses. All of the communities share meals, worship, and make community decisions on everything from doing the dishes to potential employment opportunities. For instance, members of the Sojourners community in San Francisco are discouraged from relocating for the sake of career advancement.[17] Imagine calling the community together to announce you've just been offered an incredible career move that will take you to another state, a position that will double your salary. Now imagine that the larger community advises that you should forego the opportunity so you can continue your work in the urban blighted neighborhood you're living in. If you can't imagine that, then changing where you live for the sake of the Great Commission and in the name of Jesus may be too much for you.

On the other hand,
- if the notion of making a commitment to hands-on mission work appeals to you,
- if living a life fully consistent with the New Testament is intriguing,
- if you yearn for a community that offers the potential to share your faith in both words and deeds with hundreds, yea thousands, of Wanderers and Nomads who have been sidelined by society, then perhaps you're one of the radical Hitchhikers that God is raising up for this new-old work.

It's way beyond the scope of this book and the bounds of my expertise to say much about the how-to of creating a neo-monastic community. A number of communities across the nation are willing to share what they've learned, the mistakes they've made, and the successes they've experienced. Some of these communities have existed for a decade or longer—indeed, Jesus People USA in Chicago has been around since the early 1970s. Below is a short list of neo-monastic communities that have indicated they're willing to entertain questions, visitors, interns, and even novices. Because of the ever-changing World Wide Web, I've only included the name of the community and their location—a Google search will put you in touch with them.

- Bruderhof, Rifton, New York
- Camden House, Camden, New Jersey

- Church of the Servant King, Eugene, Oregon
- Church of the Sojourners, San Francisco
- Grain of Wheat, Winnipeg
- Hope Fellowship, Waco, Texas
- Jesus People USA, ChicagoJubilee Partners, Comer, Georgia
- Koinonia Partners, Americus, Georgia
- Plow Creek Fellowship, Tiskilwa, Illinois
- Reba Place Fellowship, Evanston, Illinois
- Rutba House, Durham, North Carolina
- The Simple Way, Philadephia
- Twelve Tribes, nationwide

The Radical Conclusion

Radical evangelism is just that—radical. It demands a life change that's visible for all to see. Getting inked for Jesus. Wearing the tonsure or a habit. Relocating into the roughest part of town to be neighbors with those our culture would rather overlook.

I close with an image, a story, and comment.

In 1996, a sign appeared outside a church in Philadelphia protesting the eviction of homeless families that had taken up shelter in the abandoned building. The sign simply asked, "How can you worship a homeless man on Sunday and ignore one on Monday?" Students from Eastern University joined in the protest. As a result, two years later, the Simple Way Community was birthed by Eastern University students in the Kensington neighborhood just a few blocks from the site of the protest.[18] Radical Hitchhikers began living radical lives to be and to bring the light of the world to the darkest places.

That question will haunt the church for years to come. In the end, it will probably take more than just a handful or two of radical Hitchhikers to reach this continent for Jesus. And so I offer my own little sign:

By the Way Reflections

1. When reaching Wanderers and Nomads for Jesus, which of the following is on your "too radical" list?

- Getting a faith-based tattoo
- Wearing a habit
- Living in a neo-monastic community

- Relocating to the poorest neighborhood
- Drums in the sanctuary
- Using LCD projectors instead of hymnals
- Selling a second car to support the poor
- Wearing a Christian T-shirt or hat
- Listening to sacred hymns at church
- Listening to Christian rap at church

Wanted: 12 Christians to Change the World
Non-Radicals Need Not Apply

2. What is the most radical thing that a Christian you personally know has done for the sake of the kingdom?
3. What is the most radical thing you are willing to do to reach the Wanderers and Nomads in your community for Jesus?
4. Though radical Christians are few, they tend to make an unexpectedly significant impact on the wider church. Why do you think this is?
5. Why do you think the number of Hitchhikers willing to live as neo-monastics is rising?

NOTES

[1]Leviticus 19:19; 19:27; 20:25; 19:13; 19:19.

[2] From http://www.jimmyakin.org/2005/05/tattoo_you_and_.html.

[3]Meg Jones, "Book of Mark: Artist's Work is His Religion," *The Milwaukee Journal Sentinel,* January 25, 1999, http://www.jsonline.com/news/jan99/0125tat.asp.

[4]Joseph Scinta, personal conversation, February 8, 2006.

[5]Marisa Kakoulas, "Employment Discrimination: Be Careful What You Sue For," *Body Modification Ezine* (April 5, 2004), http://www.bmezine.com/news/guest/20040405.html.

[6]Flash is tat for the artwork created or creatable by the resident tattoo artists.

[7]Katrina Tenny-Brittian, personal conversation, January 26, 2006.

[8]Lauren F. Winner, "Eternal Ink," *Christianity Today* (October 4, 1999): 79.

[9]Certainly they went there to worship, but apparently not all at once (see Acts 3:1). Remember, too, that this option was limited to Jewish men and that it came to an abrupt end when the temple was destroyed in A.D. 70.

[10]The apostles in Jerusalem were apparently provided for, though they depended on the graciousness of patrons and donors.

[11]The desert fathers and mothers.

[12]"Number of Unchurched Adults Has Nearly Doubled Since 1991," *The Barna Report,* May 4, 2004, http://www.barna.org/FlexPage.aspx?Page=BarnaUpdate&BarnaUpdateID=1 63.

[13]Jason Byassee, "The New Monastics: Alternative Christian Communities," *The Christian Century* (October 18, 2005), http://www.christiancentury.org/article. lasso?id=1399.

[14]"The Twelve Marks of a New Monasticism," June 2004, http://www.newmonasticism. org/12marks/index.html.

[15]Jennell Paris Williams, quoted in Rob Moll, "The New Monasticism," *Christianity Today,* 49, no. 9 (September 2005): 46.

[16]Ray Bakke, *Theology as Big as the City* (Downers Grove, Ill.: InterVarsity Press, 1997), 110.

[17]Byassee, "The New Monastics."

[18]Moll, "The New Monasticism," 38.

CHAPTER EIGHT

The Ultimate Destination

We've finally arrived at the last chapter. It's been quite a journey so far, and you've been introduced to a veritable plethora of ways to share your faith with others. Some of you, however, are probably pretty confused. The book is almost complete, and I've not covered conversion, the "sinner's prayer," or even the Four Spiritual Laws. What gives?

What gives is that before you start learning techniques for "closing the sale," so-to-speak, you'd better understand the rules of the road. If you don't, you are liable to stick your thumb out and find your evangelistic efforts flattened by apathy, hostility, or worse. We don't live in our parents' world anymore, and we certainly don't live in our grandparents' world. Back in their day, evangelism techniques and programs worked well. Today, these same techniques and programs often cause more damage than they do good. It's not that our neighbors are less receptive than they once were; they're not. But they're much less receptive to the old methods we use to try to impress our faith upon them.

The Changing World

Over the years, especially with the rise of the Enlightenment and Modernity, an understanding crept into the church that mimicked the scientific culture. In science, if it can't be measured and examined in some way, then significant questions arise. That's one of the reasons faith and science so often appear to be at war with each other—you can't quantify faith or faith claims. That becomes a problem when it comes to evangelism and salvation. If you can't somehow measure it, it can't really be real, or so the logic claims. Over the past 1,500 years or so, the church inadvertently developed a way to measure faith. We called it salvation or being saved. We can be sure someone has achieved it when they pray a particular prayer. That's how we measure faith. If you've prayed "the sinner's prayer," or prayed to "accept" Jesus as your Lord and Savior, or any prayer to that effect, then you have it.

The church has measured faith this way for several hundred years or so, and that seems like a long time. However, that doesn't appear to be the only way the church has measured salvation. Let me illustrate two different ways the New Testament has "measured" salvation.

The first illustration is of Paul's conversion experience found in Acts 9. Here you find a definite moment in time when he became a Christian. Notice, however, what the biblical text *doesn't* include. It makes no mention of a specific prayer being prayed (which doesn't mean there wasn't one) or any formulaic words.

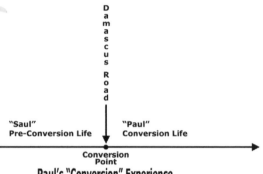

Paul's "Conversion" Experience

On the other hand, you do see an immediate response to his conversion via his baptism and receiving of the Holy Spirit.

The conversion model is clearly found in the New Testament; however, during the past 1,500 years, the church has largely embraced this as the expected experience for Christians. It isn't the only model we read about in the New Testament, though. Let's look at a second illustration.

Peter's conversion experience seems to be significantly different from Paul's. The dilemma here is to try to pinpoint when Peter "became" a Christian. Trying to pinpoint that

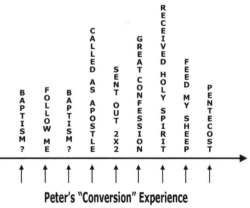

Peter's "Conversion" Experience

moment seems nearly fruitless. We don't read about Peter's baptism, so I guessed that he was probably baptized either before Jesus issued his Great Invitation to "follow me," or else he may have been baptized afterwards. The question is, though, did his baptism mark his entry into Christianity? It certainly could have, but then, Jesus hadn't died and been resurrected yet. Would that baptism count?

On the other hand, many have claimed that Peter became a Christian at the moment of his Great Confession (Mk. 8:29). However, if this is true, was Peter not a Christian when Jesus chose him to be one of his apostles? Or when he sent Peter and the other eleven (and the seventy-two) out to preach, heal, and cast out demons? You can probably see the issue here. Could Peter have been a Christian before Jesus' death and resurrection? If not, when did he become one? When Jesus bestowed the Holy Spirit upon him? When Jesus told Peter to take care of his sheep? Or was it at Pentecost in Acts 1?

The majority of those Christians born prior to 1960 can more readily relate to Peter's conversion story than Paul's. I'm one of those. I wrestled for years trying to pinpoint my own conversion moment, because "everybody" knows you need to be able to point to your spiritual birthday (that day when you were "born again," as Jesus put it to Nicodemus in John 3). But I was raised in the church. I was in church from my third Sunday outside the womb (mom would have had me there earlier, but the doctor said no). I can't recall a time in my life when I *didn't* believe that Jesus was the Christ, the Son of the Living God, and my personal Lord and Savior. I experienced no blinding light moment. I prayed no specific prayer. I was baptized when I was nine, I had a call into ministry at fourteen, I entered formal theological training when I was twenty-five, and so on. Sure, I experienced high points and some low points in my life. I relate to Peter's conversion experience, as it's outlined in the New Testament—his journey seems to be my journey too.

Indeed, I've had individuals seriously question my salvation because I couldn't point to that moment in my life when I became a Christian. A problem always arises with the logic of those who conclude that an experience they've had has to be the experience everyone else must have. Was Peter "saved" or not? My heart says yes.

Conversion Versus Conversation

Much of this book, so far, has looked at ways to get conversations about faith started. Whether you're expanding your horizons to get ENOF or heading to your local tattoo parlor to get that Celtic cross tat you've always secretly wanted, the point has been to open the doors of opportunity for having a heart-to-heart with a friend, relative, acquaintance, neighbor, coworker, or even a stranger about your faith. When you've gone to all that work to prepare the way, you probably don't want to blow the opportunity by saying the wrong thing. I realize that this is one of the reasons people hesitate to talk about their journey in the first place—fear that they won't know what to say.

The fear of the unknown has always been one of the universal fears. As we contemplate "sharing our faith" with people, we worry we'll say the wrong thing or, perhaps even worse, that we'll stumble and stutter through some presentation of the Gospel so badly that we'll look inept at best, and incompetent at worst. So we tend to just keep our mouths shut. Well, let me again relieve you of some of your anxiety. Many of our fears exist because we're still caught up in the Enlightenment mentality of conversion versus simply having a conversation. When conversion is the point of our conversation, we put too much pressure on ourselves because we unnaturally approach it as a sales call. I know that sounds harsh, but let's think through this. The goal of a conversion conversation is to get to a point where we can effectively press for a decision about Jesus:

> "Will you accept Jesus as your Lord and Savior?"
> "Will you pray with me to receive Jesus?"
> "Do you want to know for sure that if you died tonight that you'd go to heaven?"

When conversion is the goal, a great deal rides on the words we choose and the rhetoric we present. Indeed, the exact wording can seem so critical. When I was in undergraduate Bible school, our evangelism class was given a how-to book for leading people to the Lord. We had to memorize it word-for-word. Not only that, but the book included detailed instructions on how to dress, how to knock on a door appropriately, directions that included taking a step backwards when someone opened the door after we knocked (it makes you appear less intimidating), where and how to be seated in the living room, and even instructions for how to get them to turn off the television if it's a distraction.

Now, don't get me wrong. Conversion evangelism has been an effective process for many years and with many people. My personal evangelism bookshelf has dozens of how-to books that outline one plan after another for introducing people to Jesus. But, as I pointed out earlier, most of these programs and plans seldom have the desired effect in the current cultural climate. In fact, more often than not, they have the exact opposite effect. People who feel they're being sold the Gospel resent it and may conclude that "all those church people are pushy."

One thing that's lacking in the vast majority of the conversion models of evangelism is conversation. Oh sure, dialogue occurs between the evangelist and the "prospect," but it's seldom an unscripted conversation. Instead, it usually goes like this:

Evangelist: If you were to die tonight, do you know for sure you'd go to heaven?

Prospect: Well, uh, I guess not.

Evangelist: Would you like to know?

Prospect: Umm, sure.

Evangelist: Well, the Bible says that we've all sinned and fallen short of the glory of God (Rom. 3:23). That says we've all sinned. I've sinned and you've sinned. Everyone has. Like when our moms told us we couldn't have a cookie, but we snuck one anyway. We've all sinned. You've sinned in the past, haven't you?

Prospect: I, uh, I guess so.

And so it goes. Most conversion plans gently lead the seeker from wherever they are to a place where they realize they've sinned, need salvation, and can get it because of Jesus' death and resurrection. It's a carefully guided dialogue that doesn't make much allowance for authentic give-and-take conversation.

Conversation, on the other hand, is messy. It can't be scripted, which means that in some ways, the Hitchhiker has to work harder to guide it to a particular conclusion. It can be done, though. Socrates was such a master at it that they named the Socratic Method after him. The conversations he had with his students weren't scripted in advance, but with careful forethought, he was able to ask just the right questions, based on the conversation, that would lead his students to the "correct" conclusion.

I'd like to tell you that I've mastered Socrates' rhetoric and condensed it into five points so you can lead a Socratic conversation that brings people to a place where they realize they need, yea want, the guiding presence of Jesus Christ in their lives. But I've never been able to work my way through the method well enough to boil it down to those five points.

On the other hand, I think I gave up struggling through the Socratic Method because I figured there must be something more natural and more effective than micromanaging a conversation. The good news is that there is, and you've already been introduced to most of what it takes throughout this book. That more natural and more effective method is called living life on the Way. The authentic Christian life is lived on the Way. It's a Hitchhiker's paradise that can take you almost anywhere. The roads you travel and the paths you cross are scenic, filled with other Hitchhikers making their way to one destination or another. As you go, you'll brush up against some fellow journeyers and rub shoulders with others. These "touch-points" are often divine appointments, otherwise known as opportunities (see chapter 3)—opportunities to open the door to real, life-changing conversations.

Real, Life-Changing Conversations

What I've discovered, as I've hitchhiked my way through life, is that when I strike up a conversation with a fellow traveler, I almost always end up talking about the Way. Sometimes those conversations are superficial and seem (to me) to accomplish little. On the other hand, some conversations are deep enough that I get to share the reason for my hope (1 Pet. 3:15), which is to say, I get to share why I travel the Way and where that Way is taking me.

Real, life-changing conversations are like Old Faithful, the famous Yellowstone Park geyser that spouts about once an hour day in and day out. Just as the geyser springs from deep within the earth, life-changing conversations spring up from the "overflow" of our spiritual lives. Let me use an example from the New Testament: In Mark 9:14–29, nine of the disciples were trying to cast a demon out of a boy and weren't having success. When Jesus shows up, he does what the disciples weren't able to do and casts out the demon. When they asked why they weren't able to work the miracle, Jesus simply says, "This kind can come out only by prayer." Now, I've examined that passage carefully, and the scriptures don't mention Jesus praying over the boy. Indeed, when he saw the crowd rushing toward him, he got in a hurry to accomplish the deed, and simply rebuked the demon and commanded it to depart, which it did.

So what could Jesus have meant when he said "This kind only comes out by prayer," but then doesn't pray? I see two possible answers. First, we could surmise that Jesus accomplished what the disciples couldn't because he was the Son of God and had more power and authority than they, but that stands in contrast to a number of other things he taught. I'm pretty sure Jesus' command was effective because he was working from his personal "overflow." Throughout the Gospels, Jesus spends significant time in prayer. He went to the mountains, he went to the wilderness, he went alone, and he went often. Jesus had, if you will, a deep storage well filled with prayer-energy because he'd spent time in prayer days, weeks, and months before this event.

I've discovered that we all have deep storage wells in our spirit. If you spend considerable time reading and studying scripture, worshipping, praying, and practicing other spiritual disciplines including doing good works, the storage well fills up. At first, you probably won't notice anything. It's as if a gentle shower has sprinkled in the desert. But give it time. As you continue to practice spiritual habits, you'll discover that those practices inform your actions and your conversations. Your conversations will have a natural effervescence of the Spirit.

"But what do you say?" That's the main question I get from long-term church members. I suppose saying to just relax and let the conversation wander its way to where it will go is a bit vague. However, if your well is full, you really don't have to worry because the conversation will get to where it needs to go—it's a matter of trusting the Spirit. Most of us appreciate examples, instructions, and how-tos, so let me elaborate. Three preliminary steps precede a life-changing conversation.

Fill Your Storage Well

I have touched on some of the spiritual habits that will fill your well, but let me spend a few moments waxing eloquently on filling it to overflowing. Your spiritual storage well only fills when you get intentional about practicing the spiritual disciplines. I've noticed over the years that only a few people are really living their lives, even though Jesus promised his followers that we'd have a full, abundant life (Jn. 10:10). Instead, most people let life live them, that is, they do whatever the next task is that comes up without thinking about whether or not the task will make a difference in their lives. Now admittedly, some of our day-to-day tasks are difference making, but many more are just "stuff" that comes up and we tackle without reflection. Letting life live us brings up serious issues, not the least of which is that it allows the less important stuff to fill our hours. This leaves us neither the time nor the energy to take on tasks that would be truly life-changing in our own lives, let alone in the lives of others. In other words, filling your spiritual storage well isn't going to happen just because you want it to—you'll have to wrestle with how you're going to be intentional about adding a spiritual practice or two or three into your already busy life.

That's the issue I deal with in the book *High-Voltage Spirituality*. It includes over forty different spiritual practices you can add to your life.

Many of the habits are designed for beginners travelling the spiritual journey. Others suit those whose lives are so busy they have trouble figuring out how to fit God in.

When it comes to filling your spiritual storage well to overflowing, the key practice is to spend time with God. The basic underpinning of every spiritual habit/discipline/practice is prayer. Without prayer, you simply have no spiritual habits to practice. Studying the Bible without prayer is an intellectual exercise that may be interesting, but it won't feed the spirit nor fill your spiritual storage well. If you devoted your life to Bible study and did so without an intentional prayer connection, you'd starve spiritually.

On the other hand, a number of people tell me that their whole life is prayer and that they don't need to set aside time for intentional conversation with God. I could agree with that practice if it were a practical reality, but I've yet to meet a non-monastic Christian who literally spends their day in an intentional ongoing conversation with God. Most of those who "practice" this kind of prayer life actually do very little conversing with God and generally describe being aware of an emotional feeling of God's presence throughout the day. Now, it's not that being in the presence of God isn't highly desirable. It is. But sitting in the same room with someone for hours on end, or even for many days, isn't the same as having a conversation with them. Prayer is a conversation, that is, a dialogue between you and God, that could, should, and ought to take place throughout the day, at least if you're going to fill that spiritual storage well.

I need to address another prayer issue: the level of conversation. In any communication between two people three levels can be taking place. The first level is "talking about"; the second is "talking to"; and the third is "taking with."

Talking about occurs whenever two people talk about someone else. Sometimes, perhaps far too often, it's gossip. We talk about people all the time, and it isn't always a bad thing. When I tell my wife that "Sarah and Bob just gave birth to a baby girl," I'm talking about. When it comes to spirituality practices, many songs and sermons in worship talk "about" God. However, whenever we practice "talking about," we're engaging in an exclusive conversation. It leaves the object of the conversation out of the loop.

The second level of conversation is "talking to." We do a lot of this in our lives. For instance, it's perfectly okay to talk to someone when you're giving them instructions, such as when I tell my administrative assistant I'll be on the road the first two weeks in April. Teachers and preachers both talk to us to educate us. All of these are perfectly good reasons to "talk to" others. On the other hand, talking to others is often a monologue disguised as a conversation. For instance, if I'm angry or have some point I feel compelled to make, I may spend the conversation "talking to" someone. Further, many of us spend much of our lives talking to others in our regular voices rather than "talking with" them. It's just a habit. When it comes to prayer, most prayers fall into this category—we talk to God. It's a one-way "conversation." We talk, and we assume God's listening.

"Talking with" is the ultimate level of conversation and doesn't happen naturally for many people. Talking is a dialogue, but it's more than just two people talking to each other. In many conversations, dare I say most, the one being spoken to is doing less listening than they are formulating their response based on what they think they're hearing. This is perhaps the most common way we communicate with each other. We only halfway listen to what's being said because we're more focused on what we want to say. That's "talking to" disguised as a conversation.

When we "talk with" someone, we turn off our own thoughts and presuppositions to listen and comprehend what's actually being said. Not only that, we listen to how it's being said, and we listen to what's not being said as well. Good listening is hard work, even when we listen to someone who's standing right in front us and with whom we are agreeing. Talking with God is the ultimate level of prayer as well—and it's the only level that fills up our spiritual storage wells. Talking with God means prayer that's a real dialogue. It means talking *and* listening. It means listening with our own biases and thoughts set aside so we can comprehend and discern what God wants for our lives.

All that's to say this: the prayer that will fill your spiritual storage well doesn't just happen. It's intentional! At first it's not natural, at least for most of us. But the good news is that if you'll make it a priority, it will become easier and maybe even second nature.

Answer the Ultimate Question

Back in chapter 1, you dealt with the question, "What is it about your experience with Jesus that your neighbors, your community, your world cannot live without?" This is just one of several questions that cannot help you answer the ultimate question Peter presupposes in 1 Peter 3:15, "Always be prepared to give an answer to everyone who asks you the reason for the hope that you have" (TNIV). Peter presupposes that we, as Hitchhikers on the Way, are going to meet people who will naturally ask "So, what makes you so different from everyone else around here?" People only ask that kind of question to someone whose life is *radically* different from everyone else's lives, and your life *will* be radically different from others if you're being intentional about filling your spiritual storage well to overflowing. When someone asks that question, or when it comes up in conversation, you need to have something life-changing to say. If you haven't ever given much thought to the ultimate question, though, you may be at a loss for words.

The answer to the ultimate question, however, is less about writing an essay than about discovering what's already within you. If you set out to create your "testimony," it will likely sound and feel contrived. The answer to the ultimate question is a part of who you are, not a statement you regurgitate on an essay test. Depending on who you are, it could be a story from your past; it could be an image you've adopted that communicates your commitment; it could be a talisman that you carry that triggers an emotion or an account of your life; or it could even be a carefully thought out response generated from your experiences. Regardless of the "how," the answer to the ultimate question will move, touch, and inspire others when you share from your passion.

To find the answer to the ultimate question, though, you will probably need to take some prayerful time to reflect on the question, just what is the reason for your hope? You might find some help in answering the ultimate question by pondering one or more of these:

- What is it about your experience with Jesus that's changing your life?
- What was your life like before you encountered Jesus and committed to follow him and what is it like now?
- What are you hearing from God in your prayer time? How is that informing and enriching your life?
- In what events of your life have you noticed the fingerprints of the Spirit intervening all over the place?
- How has your relationship with Jesus given meaning to your life?

You will need to spend significant time with these questions before you're ready to tackle the answer to the ultimate question of what it is about your relationship with Jesus that the world can't live without. In our hustle-bustle world, we often discover that we simply don't have the time, or that we won't prioritize the time, to do the reflecting necessary to make a difference.

As I said earlier, few people actually live their lives; most of us allow life to live us. Most of us wake up in the morning and go through the same routine we did the day before because that's just the way it is. Some of it is habit, but much more of it is mindlessness. We do what we do because it's what we do. Frankly, the majority of Christians (or people, for that matter) come to be slightly on the lazy side. We take the path of least resistance. We end up in the jobs we end up with, rather than pursuing the dreams God gave us. Rather than making waves at work (or home or church or …), we compromise our values to maintain the status quo of what's comfortable. We're more interested in maintaining harmony than we are in pursuing what's right. It's so much easier to just "be" than it is to be different. That's why it's so important to take time to stop and reflect.

Reflecting on our lives overall has value, if you want your life to make a difference. If you want to live life rather than letting it live you, then you're going to have to make the time to reflect on what you did *today,* and you'll have to do it again tomorrow and the next day and the next. When you do, your life will begin to change in subtle and not-so-subtle ways. You'll begin to choose the important over the urgent. You'll find the time to ponder the ultimate question, to really ponder it and refine your answer.

Have a Conversation

When your spiritual storage well is full and you've discovered the answer to the ultimate question, then it's time to have a conversation or two or a couple hundred. First, let me say that if you've actually accomplished these two steps, you won't need to read this section because the conversations will naturally spring up. It's just the way the Spirit works.

However, during a spiritual conversation many of us tend to revert to Modernism and try to convince, argue, or even explain the faith. That may have worked once, but by and large, it isn't effective faith sharing today. Instead, our conversation partner will take up a defensive position as we begin our persuasive conversation. At that point, pretty much all is lost. Almost no one is "convinced" into the kingdom. That's why Peter's question is so important and so relevant today—the question is ultimately about our relationship with Jesus. In a conversation, if you try to be "persuasive," someone can discount anything you say. For instance, you say, "The Bible says …" and they may respond, "So what? The Bible is just another book." From that point on, you can try all you want to convince them, but your conversation will simply reinforce their assumptions about Christianity in general, and Christians specifically. It's a lose-lose proposition.

On the other hand, if you share your story, if you share the reason for your hope, if you share from your overflow, the conversation will be different. Instead of "The Bible says ..." propositional statements, you'll be sharing your heart. Instead of relying on what you've learned, you'll be sharing experiences that are making a real difference in your life. Now that's interesting and inspiring and motivating. There's no better advertisement than a satisfied customer, and there's no better witness for Jesus than a changed life. That's why you must spend the time reflecting on your own life and your own reason for the hope.

The Invitation

It's one thing to have a conversation about your faith. It's quite another to have a life-changing conversation. The difference between the two can be summed up in one words: Invitation. Let's face it, we have conversations with people all day long. Though most of them may be pleasant, few of them change our lives. Those that do have a couple things in common.

First, life-changing conversations are inspirational. They ring true and "jazz" us. They stir our souls and excite our imaginations. They give us hope. Second, life-changing conversations are personal, interactive, and, well, conversational, that is, they're dialogue rather than monologue. Listening is a necessary part of conversation, especially life-changing ones. Finally, life-changing conversations come with either an implicit or an explicit invitation to do something. If the conversation doesn't have an invitation, although it may be inspiring and make you feel all warm and fuzzy inside, it won't change your life because it's little more than informational. Our lives change only when we do something different with our lives. What we know "about" makes virtually no real-life difference. Only when we put something into practice, when we begin behaving differently, does life change occur. That means, for those of us initiating a life-changing conversation, we need to offer a life-changing invitation.

What might you offer? You can choose from many possibilities. You could offer to pray with them. You could offer to help hold them accountable for some life-changing spiritual habit they want to practice. You could offer to do a Bible study with them. You could offer to be a spiritual mentor or guide for them. You could invite them to your life-changing small group or life-changing church event.

On the other hand, please do not invite people with whom you've shared your faith to a small group or a church event that isn't transformational; disciple making is too important, and these relationships too tenuous, to invite them into anything as potentially destructive as an unhealthy congregation. Those you've inspired need to be invited into a nurturing community that takes disciple making seriously, so be selective about what the invitation you make. But once you've made the invitation, it's pretty much up to them and their response to the nudging of the Spirit.

Don't rest all your hopes on a single conversation. If you're friends with your conversational partner, the conversation you've had will continue. You'll have the opportunity to make other invitations. The key word is continue. Keep the conversation going and, though you shouldn't be annoying, keep making invitations. Remember, it's a conversation that invites them to a changed life. That's the point of evangelism—to share the good news and invite others to join you on the Way.

Epilogue

I've been a Hitchhiker as long as I can remember, and I've been a lot of places as I've traveled the Way. Sometimes I'm on the straight and narrow, and there have been times I've made my own detours through the less savory places of life. But I've always returned, because I've discovered that traveling with Jesus is what makes life worth living.

My prayer is that through the words of this book, you've found a kindred spirit to travel with—no, not me, but rather someone you know who's wandering through life and unclear about where life is heading. If you don't know any Wanderers, I pray you've been inspired to rectify this shortcoming. No follower of Jesus Christ can be faithful to the teachings of Jesus, and in particular to the Great Commission, without being intentional in relationships with unbelievers, the unchurched, and the never churched: those whom you've come to know as the Wanderers and the Nomads.

And so I bid you safe travels as you continue your journey. Who knows…perhaps our paths may cross sometime on the Way. If you'd like to make a connection, please don't hesitate to stop by. You can find me hanging out with Wanderers and Nomads at some Starbucks or chatting with fellow Hitchhikers at www.HitchhikersGuideToEvangelism.com.

APPENDIX A

The Names of Jesus

Advocate (1 John 2:1)
Almighty (Revelation 1:8)
Alpha and Omega (Revelation 22:13)
Amen (Revelation 3:14)
Apostle of Our Confession (Hebrews 3:1)
Atoning Sacrifice for Our Sins (1 John 2:2)
Author of Life (Acts 3:15)
Author and Perfecter of Our Faith (Hebrews 12:2)
Author of Salvation (Hebrews 2:10)
Beginning and End (Revelation 22:13)
Blessed and Only Ruler (1 Timothy 6:15)
Bread of God (John 6:33)
Bread of Life (John 6:35)
Bridegroom (Matthew 9:15)
Capstone (Acts 4:11)
Chief Cornerstone (Ephesians 2:20)
Chief Shepherd (1 Peter 5:4)
Christ (1 John 2:22)
Creator (John 1:3)
Deliverer (Romans 11:26)
Eternal Life (1 John 1:2)
Faithful and True (Revelation 19:11)
Faithful Witness (Revelation 1:5)
Faith and True Witness (Revelation 3:14)
First and Last (Revelation 1:17)
Firstborn from the Dead (Revelation 1:5)
Firstborn over All Creation (Colossians 1:15)
Gate (John 10:9)
God (John 20:28)
Good Shepherd (John 10:11, 14)
Great Shepherd (Hebrews 13:20)
Great High Priest (Hebrews 4:14)
Head of the Church (Ephesians 1:22)
Healer (Acts 9:34)
Heir of all things (Hebrews 1:2)

High Priest (Hebrews 2:17)
Holy and True (Revelation 3:7)
Holy One (Acts 3:14)
Hope (1 Timothy 1:1)
Hope of Glory (Colossians 1:27)
Horn of Salvation (Luke 1:69)
I Am (John 8:58)
Image of God (2 Corinthians 4:4)
Immanuel (Matthew 1:23)
Judge of the Living and the Dead (Acts 10:42)
King Eternal (1 Timothy 1:17)
King of Israel (John 1:49)
King of the Jews (Matthew 27:11)
King of Kings (Revelation 19:16)
King of the Ages (Revelation 15:3)
Lamb (Revelation 13:8)
Lamb of God (John 1:29)
Lamb without Blemish (1 Peter 1:19)
Last Adam (1 Corinthians 15:45)
Life (John 14:6; Colossians 3:4)
Light of the World (John 8:12)
Lion of the Tribe of Judah (Revelation 5:5)
Living One (Revelation 1:18)
Living Stone (1 Peter 2:4)
Lord (2 Peter 2:20)
Lord of All (Acts 10:36)
Lord of Glory (1 Corinthians 2:8)
Lord of Lords (Revelation 19:16)
Man from Heaven (1 Corinthians 15:48)
Mediator of the New Covenant (Hebrews 9:15)
Morning Star (Revelation 22:16)
Offspring of David (Revelation 22:16)
Only Begotten Son of God (John 1:18)
Our Great God and Savior (Titus 2:13)
Our Holiness (1 Corinthians 1:30)
Our Husband (2 Corinthians 11:2)
Our Protection (2 Thessalonians 3:3)
Our Redemption (1 Corinthians 1:30)
Our Righteousness (1 Corinthians 1:30)
Our Sacrificed Passover Lamb (1 Corinthians 5:7)

Power of God (1 Corinthians 1:24)
Precious Cornerstone (1 Peter 2:6)
Prophet (Acts 3:22)
Protector (2 Thessalonians 3:3)
Rabbi (Matthew 26:25)
Resurrection and Life (John 11:25)
Righteous One (Acts 7:52)
Rock (1 Corinthians 10:4)
Root of David (Revelation 5:5)
Ruler of God's Creation (Revelation 3:14)
Ruler of the Kings of the Earth (Revelation 1:5)
Savior (Ephesians 5:23)
Son of David (Luke 18:39)
Son of God (John 1:49)
Son of Man (Matthew 8:20)
Son of the Most High God (Luke 1:32)
Source of Eternal Salvation (Hebrews 5:9)
The One Mediator (1 Timothy 2:5)
The Stone the Builders Rejected (Acts 4:11)
True Bread (John 6:32)
True Light (John 1:9)
True Vine (John 15:1)
Truth (John 1:14; 14:6)
Way (John 14:6)
Wisdom of God (1 Corinthians 1:24)
Word (John 1:1)
Word of God (Revelation 19:13)

APPENDIX B

The One-Anothers for the Church

–Salt is good, but if it loses its saltiness, how can you make it salty again? Have salt in yourselves, and be at peace with each other. (Mark 9:50)

–A new command I give you: Love one another. As I have loved you, so you must love one another. By this everyone will know that you are my disciples, if you love one another. (John 13:34–35)

–My command is this: Love each other as I have loved you. (John 15:12)

–This is my command: Love each other. (John 15:17)

–Be devoted to one another in love. Honor one another above yourselves. (Romans 12:10)

–Live in harmony with one another. Do not be proud, but be willing to associate with people of low position. Do not think you are superior. (Romans 12:16)

–Let no debt remain outstanding, except the continuing debt to love one another, for whoever loves others has fulfilled the law. (Romans 13:8)

–Therefore let us stop passing judgment on one another. Instead, make up your mind not to put any stumbling block or obstacle in the way of a brother or sister. (Romans 14:13)

–Accept one another, then, just as Christ accepted you, in order to bring praise to God. (Romans 15:7)

–I myself am convinced, my brothers and sisters, that you yourselves are full of goodness, filled with knowledge and competent to instruct one another. (Romans 15:14)

–Greet one another with a holy kiss. (Romans 16:16)

–I appeal to you, brothers and sisters, in the name of our Lord Jesus Christ, that all of you agree with one another in what you say and that there be no divisions among you, but that you be perfectly united in mind and thought. (1 Corinthians 1:10)

–So then, my brothers and sisters, when you gather to eat, you should all eat together. (1 Corinthians 11:33)

– So that there should be no division in the body, but that its parts should have equal concern for each other. (1 Corinthians 12:25)

– You, my brothers and sisters, were called to be free. But do not use your freedom to indulge the sinful nature; rather, serve one another humbly in love. (Galatians 5:13)

– Be completely humble and gentle; be patient, bearing with one another in love. (Ephesians 4:2)

– Be kind and compassionate to one another, forgiving each other, just as in Christ God forgave you. (Ephesians 4:32)

– Speaking to one another with psalms, hymns and songs from the Spirit. Sing and make music from your heart to the Lord, (Ephesians 5:19)

– Submit to one another out of reverence for Christ. (Ephesians 5:21)

– Bear with each other and forgive one another if any of you has a grievance against someone. Forgive as the Lord forgave you. (Colossians 3:13)

– Let the message of Christ dwell among you richly as you teach and admonish one another with all wisdom through psalms, hymns and songs from the Spirit, singing to God with gratitude in your hearts. (Colossians 3:16)

– Therefore encourage one another and build each other up, just as in fact you are doing. (1 Thessalonians 5:11)

– Hold them in the highest regard in love because of their work. Live in peace with each other. (1 Thessalonians 5:13)

– Make sure that nobody pays back wrong for wrong, but always strive to do what is good for each other and for everyone else. (1 Thessalonians 5:15)

– But encourage one another daily, as long as it is called "Today," so that none of you may be hardened by sin's deceitfulness. (Hebrews 3:13)

– And let us consider how we may spur one another on toward love and good deeds, not giving up meeting together, as some are in the habit of doing, but encouraging one another—and all the more as you see the Day approaching. (Hebrews 10:24–25)

– Keep on loving one another as brothers and sisters. (Hebrews 13:1)

–Brothers and sisters, do not slander one another. Anyone who speaks against a brother or sister or judges them speaks against the law and judges it. When you judge the law, you are not keeping it, but sitting in judgment on it. (James 4:11)

–Therefore confess your sins to each other and pray for each other so that you may be healed. The prayer of a righteous person is powerful and effective. (James 5:16)

–Now that you have purified yourselves by obeying the truth so that you have sincere love for each other, love one another deeply, from the heart. (1 Peter 1:22)

–Finally, all of you, be like-minded, be sympathetic, love one another, be compassionate and humble. (1 Peter 3:8)

–Above all, love each other deeply, because love covers over a multitude of sins. (1 Peter 4:8)

–Offer hospitality to one another without grumbling. (1 Peter 4:9)

–In the same way, you who are younger, submit yourselves to your elders. All of you, clothe yourselves with humility toward one another, because, "God opposes the proud but shows favor to the humble and oppressed." (1 Peter 5:5)

–But if we walk in the light, as he is in the light, we have fellowship with one another, and the blood of Jesus, his Son, purifies us from all sin. (1 John 1:7)

–For this is the message you heard from the beginning: We should love one another. (1 John 3:11)

–And this is his command: to believe in the name of his Son, Jesus Christ, and to love one another as he commanded us. (1 John 3:23)

–Dear friends, let us love one another, for love comes from God. Everyone who loves has been born of God and knows God. (1 John 4:7)

–Dear friends, since God so loved us, we also ought to love one another. No one has ever seen God; but if we love one another, God lives in us and his love is made complete in us. (1 John 4:11–12)

–And now, dear lady, I am not writing you a new command but one we have had from the beginning. I ask that we love one another. (2 John 1:5)

APPENDIX C

The Discovery Questions

1. **What did you like about what you read?**
   What was the best part of the reading? Did you discover a new insight? Was something particularly helpful?
2. **What did you *not* like about what you read?**
   What was the most disturbing part of the reading? Did something bother you? What was "hard to hear"?
3. **What did you not understand about what you read?**
   Did something confuse you or not make sense? Who can you chat with about this or where can you go to get clarification?
4. **What did you learn about God or the Kingdom of God?**
   How are God's ways different than our ways? How is Kingdom living different than living outside of the Kingdom? How is your "image of God" different than it was before?
5. **What is God calling you to do and what are you going to do about it?**
   Is there something for you to do? Is there a misdeed to confess, repent of, and make amends for? Do you have an addiction God is prompting you to release? Do you have an attitude that needs an adjustment? How will you move from thought to action?
6. **What verse, phrase, word, or thought do you want to take away with you?**
   What do you want to remember through your day? Is there something you want to tuck away into the back of your mind and muse over? What part of the reading will make a difference in the way you live today?

APPENDIX D

Opening the Door for the Romans Road

Originally, the Romans Road was used in door-to-door evangelism. Indeed, I used it almost daily when I was in college and on staff of a new church in the South. I went from house to house with a survey designed for two purposes. First, I used the survey to identify prospective Nomads—believers who were not attached to a local church. When I found one, I would leave literature on the new church and invite them to come. The second purpose of the survey was to identify Wanderers and to see if they were "ripe" and ready to make a commitment to Jesus. (This style of evangelism takes seriously the belief that the Holy Spirit is working in people's lives even without our personal input—John 4:34–38). If I didn't find a spiritual inquirer, a rare circumstance in the area we were planting the church, I planted a few seeds. If, however, I found any sign of a spiritual wanderer at all, then I would steer the conversation along a spiritual path to see if a harvest could be had. What follows is the script I used to introduce the Romans Road.

Do you ever give much thought to spiritual things?

> *This was one of the questions on the survey. No matter what the answer is, I would move on to the next question.*

What do you think it takes to get to heaven?

> *If the answer is anything besides "Invite Jesus as my Lord and Savior" then continue.*

Yes, those are important things for all our lives, but could I show you what the Bible says about what it takes to get to heaven?

> *If they said no or put me off, I would leave literature about the church that included more about needing a relationship with Jesus. Then I'd invite them to visit the church sometime, thank them, and leave.*

> *If they said yes, then I would continue by traveling the Romans Road with them. There are many versions that you can find via Google to fill in any gaps. What follows is a shorthand version of theThe Romans Road:*

Romans 3:23. "For all have sinned and fall short of the glory of God."

> *Whenever it's possible, get them to read the passage. There's something*

powerful about reading the Bible. Then go on with something like,

"This verse says that everybody has sinned. I've sinned, you've sinned, everybody has sinned. Did you ever disobey your mom or dad? Sure, we've all done some things we're not proud of. The verse also says we've fallen short of God's glory. God's glory is Jesus, the only one who never sinned. I know I'm not as good as Jesus. Why, even Mother Teresa said she wasn't as good as Jesus."

Romans 6:23a. "For the wages of sin is death...."

"This verse reminds us that there are consequences for everything we do. If you work at a job for eight hours, you expect to get paid for eight hours, don't you? And if you refused to pay your water bill, though you wouldn't like it, you'd expect that they would come and turn it off, right? Well, sin is like that. Except the consequence of sin is death. The Bible teaches there are two kinds of death. One is the death of the body, and the other is a spiritual death. Spiritual death means being separated from God. Our sin pushes God away, but that's not what God had in mind. God wants to be in a healthy relationship with us. But we've sinned, so there's that consequence that has to be dealt with. It's as if we have an outstanding debt that has to paid."

Romans 5:8. "But God demonstrates his own love for us in this: While we were still sinners, Christ died for us."

"Here the Bible tells us that God didn't just talk about love, but demonstrated it. Even though we had a debt we owed, Jesus came and paid the price of death to pay it off—even though he was the only one who's never sinned, he paid the consequence. He paid a debt he didn't owe so we wouldn't have to pay it."

Romans 6:23b. "...but the gift of God is eternal life in Christ Jesus our Lord."

"God loves us so much that Jesus was willing to pay the price so we could have eternal life. But then Jesus did something that's never been done. Jesus didn't stay dead. God resurrected him from the dead to show us the truth about eternal life. God's gift means there's nothing that separates us from God, not even death. But like any gift, it comes with a choice. We can choose to receive the gift, or we can reject it. Jesus isn't going to force himself on us."

Romans 10:9–10. "If you confess with your mouth, 'Jesus is Lord,' and believe in your heart that God raised him from the dead, you will be saved. For it is with your heart that you believe and are justified, and it is with your mouth that you confess and are saved."

This is the critical point, the moment when you are going to ask the ultimate question, "Are you ready to ask Jesus to be your Lord and to become your life's guide?"

"These are the verses that tell us how to receive the gift. It says you first have to believe in God. And you have to believe that Jesus paid the price by his death and that he beat death by his resurrection. Do you believe Jesus died and was resurrected?"

Wait for a response. If yes, then proceed.

"You also have to invite Jesus to be the Lord of your life—that means you trust him to be your life-leader and guide. Are you ready to start living an eternal life with Jesus as your life-leader and guide?"

Wait for a response. If yes, then proceed.

Romans 10:13. "For everyone who calls on the name of the Lord will be saved."

"Verse 13 invites us to ask Jesus for the gift he offers—asking him to renew your mind, transform you life, and be your Lord and your guide. To do that you just call on Jesus in prayer. Would you like to ask Jesus to give you eternal life, to be your life-leader and guide?"

If they say yes, then bow your head and pray a prayer like the following, asking your friend to repeat after you:

"Jesus, I believe in you. I believe you died and that you beat death by your resurrection. Come into my life and renew my mind. Remove all my sin. Come be my life-leader and my guide. I will follow you. Thank you for your gift of life. Amen."

What happens next is probably more important than what has just transpired. New believers who don't stick their thumbs out to begin a faith journey with the Spirit and in the company of other hitchhikers are going to find themselves going nowhere fast. You might want to invite the new believer to an existing Bible study or small group, if you're a part of one that is life transforming. You could offer to start a discipleship or Bible study with the person and his or her friends. Certainly, it's a good time to talk about living the Christian life as a disciple of Jesus and that baptism is one of the first instructions Jesus gave to new followers. No matter how you phrase it or what you invite them to, traveling the Romans Road is a dead end if in the end it doesn't lead to discipleship.

Works Cited

"2004 American Community Survey: Data Profile Highlights," U.S. Census Bureau, http://factfinder.census.gov/servlet/ACSSAFFFacts?_event=&geo_id=01000US&_geoContext=01000US&_street=&_county=&_cityTown=&_state=&_zip=&_lang=en&_sse=on&ActiveGeoDiv=&_useEV=&pctxt=fph&pgsl=010.

"A Sperm Whale." *Hitchhiker's Guide to the Galaxy*, DVD. Directed by Garth Jennings (Burbank, Calif., 2005).

"A Vroom with a View." *House2House* 6 (2002): 34.

Bakke, Ray. *As Big as the City*. Downers Grove, Illinois: InterVarsity Press, 1997.

Byassee, Jason. "The New Monastics: Alternative Christian Communities." *The Christian Century Magazine* (October 18, 2005.) http://www.christiancentury.org/article.lasso?id=1399.

Chapman, Steven Curtis. "Let Us Pray." *Sign of Life*. Sparrow/EMD, B000005KYA, and EMI Christian Publishing, 1996.

"Church Planting: Get Out There," ChurchPlantingVillage.Net,. http://www.churchplantingvillage.net/site/c.iiJTKZPEJpH/b.848885/k.A7A6/Get_Out_There.htm.

Eldredge, John. *Epic: The Story God Is Telling and the Role That Is Yours to Play*. Nashville: Thomas Nelson, 2004.

_____. *Wild at Heart: Discovering the Passionate Soul of a Man*. Nashville: Thomas Nelson, 2001.

Fox, Jack. "Marketing in a Time-Scarce World," *SmartPros*. (June 2002). http://accounting.smartpros.com/x34381.xml.

Gladwell, Malcolm. *The Tipping Point: How Little Things Can Make a Big Difference*. New York: Little, Brown & Co., 2002.

Holmes, Thomas, and Richard Rahe. "Social Readjustment Rating Scale." *Journal of Psychosomatic Research* 11, no. 2 (1967).

"How Many People Go Regularly to Weekly Religious Services?," Ontario Consultants on Religious Tolerance. http://www.religioustolerance.org/rel_rate.htm.

Hybels, Bill, and Mark Mittelberg. *Becoming a Contagious Christian*. Nashville: Zondervan, 1994.

Jones, Meg. "Book of Mark: Artist's Work Is His Religion," *The Milwaukee Journal Sentinel*, January 25, 1999. http://www.jsonline.com/news/jan99/0125tat.asp.

Kakoulas, Marisa. "Employment Discrimination: Be Careful What You Sue For." *Body Modification Ezine*, April 5, 2004. http://www.bmezine.com/news/guest/20040405.html.

Lampman, Jane. "New Thirst for Spirituality Being Felt Worldwide." *The Christian Science Monitor*. http://www.csmonitor.com/cgi-bin/wit_article.pl?script/98/11/25/112598.feat.feat.17.

Lester, Betty. "A Little Instrument." *TheChristianOnlineMagazine. Com*, 2004. 42281%7CCHID147904%7CCIID1739238. http://206.112.70.75/CC/article/0, PTID42281%7CCHID147904%7CCIID1739238, 00.html.

Mayer, Egon, Barry A. Kosmin, and Ariela Keysar. *American Religious Identification Survey*. New York: Graduate Center of the City of New York University, 2001. http://www.gc.cuny.edu/faculty/research_briefs/aris/key_findings.htm.

Moll, Rob. "The New Monasticism." *Christianity Today* 49, no. 9 (September 2005): 46.

"Number of Unchurched Adults Has Nearly Doubled Since 1991," *The Barna Report* (May 4, 2004). http://www.barna.org/FlexPage.aspx?Page=BarnaUpdate&BarnaUpdateID=163.

Peet, Mary. "Tomato: Harvest and Post-Harvest." In *Sustainable Practices for Vegetable Production in the South*. North Carolina State University. http://www.cals.ncsu.edu/sustainable/peet/profiles/harv_tom.html.

Poole, Garry. *The Complete Book of Questions: 1001 Conversation Starters for Any Occasion*. Grand Rapids, Mich: Zondervan, 2003.

Rainer, Thom S. *Surprising Insights from the Unchurched*. Grand Rapids: Zondervan, 2001.

_____. *The Unchurched Next Door*. Grand Rapids: Zondervan, 2003.

Sjogren, Steve. *Conspiracy of Kindness*. Ann Arbor: Vine Books, 1993.

_____. *101 Ways to Reach Your Community*. Colorado Springs: NavPress, 2001.

"Surveys Show Pastors Claim Congregants Are Deeply Committed to God But Congregants Deny It!" *The Barna Update* (January 9, 2006). http://www.barna.org/FlexPage.aspx?Page=BarnaUpdateNarrow&BarnaUpdateID=206.

The Apostolic Traditions of Hippolytus of Rome. Translated by Kevin P. Edgecomb (2000). http://www.bombaxo.com/hippolytus.html.

"The Twelve Marks of a New Monasticism." *New Monasticism.org*, June 2004. http://www.newmonasticism.org/12marks/index.html.

Williams, Carla. *As You Walk Along the Way.* Camp Hill, Pa.: Horizon Books, 2001.

Winner, Lauren F. "Eternal Ink." *Christianity Today* 79 (October 4, 1999).